"RELICS OF THE DHARMAKAYA" BY ONTRUL TENPA'I WANGCHUK

A DETAILED EXPLANATION OF THE THREE LINES THAT STRIKE THE KEY POINTS

BY TONY DUFF
PADMA KARPO TRANSLATION COMMITTEE

This text is secret and should not be shown to those who have not had the necessary introduction and instructions of the Thorough Cut system of Dzogchen meditation. If you have not had the necessary instructions, reading this text can be harmful to your spiritual health! Seal! Seal! Seal!

First edition, October 10th, 2010
ISBN: 978-9937-8386-2-7

Janson typeface with diacritical marks and
Tibetan Classic typeface
Designed and created by Tony Duff
Tibetan Computer Company
http://www.tibet.dk/tcc

Produced, Printed, and Published by
Padma Karpo Translation Committee
P.O. Box 4957
Kathmandu
NEPAL

Web-site and e-mail contact through:
http://www.tibet.dk/pktc
or search Padma Karpo Translation Committee on the web.

CONTENTS

INTRODUCTION

This book presents the practice called Thorough Cut, one of the two main practices of the Nyingthig or quintessential level of Dzogchen or Great Completion practice. There are several key teachings on Thorough Cut within this quintessential level of teaching, one of them being the teaching given by Garab Dorje called "The Three Lines that Strike the Key Points". There are, in turn, various explanations of the Three Lines teaching. For example, in the Longchen Nyingthig system, there is a short one by Dza Patrul, called *Feature of the Expert Glorious King*, which has become very popular. This book contains a detailed explanation of Dza Patrul's text written by Ontrul Tenpa'i Wangchuk, who is widely regarded within Tibet as the greatest master of Great Completion alive in Tibet today. His commentary, called *"Relics of Dharmakaya", Notes on the Three Lines that Strike the Key Points Compiled from the Words of my Glorious Holy Guru*, is the most detailed commentary to Dza Patrul's text that has been written to date.

The Meaning of Great Completion

The Great Completion system of dharma came from a land called Uddiyana, which is thought to have been in what is now the Swat region of Pakistan. The name of the system of dharma in the language of Uddiyana was "mahāsandhi". The name mahāsandhi means exactly "the great juncture" and refers to the one all-encompassing space in which all that there could be—whether enlightened or unenlightened, whether belonging to nirvana or samsara—is present.

The Tibetans translated this name as "rdzogs pa chen po". The term "chen po" is the exact equivalent of "mahā" and means "great" in English. The term "rdzogs pa" is not exactly equivalent to "sandhi" because its literal meaning is "a state of completion" rather than "a juncture". However, it was chosen in this case because one of its meanings, "a situation in which everything is present", does match the meaning of "sandhi". In the terminology of the original Tibetan translators, "chen po" is a literal translation and "rdzogs pa" is a meaning translation.

When this name is translated into English from the Uddiyanian term, it comes out to "Great Juncture" in both literal and meaning styles of translation. However, when translated from the Tibetan term, it comes out to "Great Completion" in literal translation and "Great Juncture" in meaning translation. Although the English translation "Great Completion" is used nowadays because of following the Tibetan wording literally, I think we should start using "Great Juncture" because it both translates the term literally and conveys the meaning intended. Nonetheless, for this book I have continued to use "Great Completion" in order to avoid confusion.

This exercise in arriving at a correct translation of the name is not done merely as an exercise in translation. It is done to bring out the great meaning embodied in the name. Great Completion refers to an all-inclusive space that beings, including humans, could realize. It is also used to refer to the system of instruction designed to bring them to an all-inclusive realization of that space. When a being does realize it, there is nothing more to be realized or done because all is complete within that being's space of realization and the work of spiritual practice is complete. In a Buddhist way of talking, Great Completion is the final realization in which that being has manifested true and complete buddhahood.

Great Completion is often called "Great Perfection" in English but that presents an incorrect understanding of the name. The final space of realization is not a state of perfection but one that contains both perfection and imperfection. The name should not connect us to the idea of perfection but to the idea of the juncture of all things perfect and imperfect, to the idea of a state of realization in which all things are complete. There is also the problem that "Great Perfection" feeds into the theistic habits of the West. It easily misleads people into thinking of a godly state of perfection.

There is also the unavoidable point that Longchen Rabjam's definitive explanations in his revered text *The Dharmadhatu Treasury* make it clear beyond a doubt that the meaning of the name is Great Completion and not Great Perfection. He mentions in several places that the point of the name is the inclusion—just as the original name from Uddiyana states—of all dharmas within dharmadhatu wisdom.

You might ask what the "great" in the name means. It does not mean that this is a "fantastic" or "wonderful" state of completion, a meaning that comes to many people based on the slang use of "great". In the Buddhist tantras, this term is used to distinguish something known by wisdom in direct perception from the same thing known by dualistic mind as a concept. In other words, *Great* Completion does not refer to the lesser state of completion understood through the use of concept but to the great version of that, the actual state of completion known through wisdom.

The Meaning of Nyingthig Great Completion

The Great Completion teaching is the ultimate of all Buddhist teachings though it has within it several, increasingly profound levels of teaching. The most profound level of teaching has an Indian name which literally says "heart's drop" but means "quintessential". It was translated into Tibetan as "nyingthig"[1] which also literally says "heart's drop" but means "quintessential". Thus, Nyingthig Great Completion is the name for the quintessential level of Great Completion teaching. This level is also called "innermost"and "unsurpassable" with the same meaning.

---

[1] Tib. snying gi thig le. The word "thig le" is also written in Tibetan as "tig le" with no difference in meaning.

The Meaning of Thorough Cut

The quintessential or Nyingthig level of Great Completion teaching has two main practices. The first is called "threg-cho" in the Tibetan language, which literally translates as Thorough Cut; the second is called "thogal" which translates as Direct Crossing. This book is concerned only with Thorough Cut practice.

The meaning of Thorough Cut practice is clearly explained in the *Illuminator Tibetan-English Dictionary*[2]:

> "Thorough Cut is a practice that slices through the solidification produced by rational mind as it grasps at a perceived object and perceiving subject. It is done in order to get to the underlying reality which is always present in the core of mind and which is called Alpha Purity in this system of teachings. For this reason, Thorough Cut is also known as Alpha Purity Thorough Cut."

The etymology of the word is explained in the Great Completion teachings with both ཁྲེགས་སུ་ཆོད་པ་ (khregs su chod pa) and ཁྲེགས་གེ་ཆོད་པ་ (khregs ge chod pa). In either case, the term ཆོད་པ་ (chod pa) means"a cut"; there are all sorts of different "cuts" and this is one of them. In the first explanation, ཁྲེགས་སུ་ (khregs su) is an adverb modifying the verb "to cut" and

[2] Published by Padma Karpo Translation Committee; see the web-site listed on the copyright page.

has the meaning of making the cut fully, completely. It is traditionally explained with the example of slicing off a finger. A finger could be sliced with a sharp knife such that the cut was not quite complete or the finger could be sliced through in one, decisive movement such that it was completely and definitely severed. That kind of complete cut is what is meant here. In the second explanation, the term ཁྲེགས་གེ་ (khregs ge) is an adverb that has the meaning of something that is doubtless, of something that is unquestionably so. A "decisive cut" is what is meant here. Thorough Cut is an excellent fit for both explanations.

Other translations that have been put forward for this term are: "Cutting Resistance" and "Cutting Solidity". Both are grammatically incorrect. Further, the name "Cutting Resistance" is made on the basis of students expressing resistance to practice and the like, but that is not the meaning intended. Similarly, the name Cutting Solidity comes from not understanding that the term ཁྲེགས་ (khregs) has both old and new meanings; the newer meaning of "solid", "solidity" does not apply because the term Thorough Cut was put into use in the time of Padmasaṃbhava when only the old meaning of ཁྲེགས་ was in use. The term means that the practitioner of this system cuts *decisively* through rational mind, regardless of its degree of solidity, so as to arrive directly at the essence of mind.

The "Three Lines That Strike the Key Points" Teaching of Thorough Cut

One of the most important teachings on Thorough Cut comes from the first human holder of the Great Completion teachings in this world, Garab Dorje of India. He gave a particular teaching on Thorough Cut called "The Three Lines that Strike the Key Points" to his main disciple Manjushrimitra.

This teaching was passed from Manjushrimitra to Shri Singha. After that it was passed to Padmasambhava and Vimalamitra, both of whom took it into Tibet. In Tibet, it went on from Padmasambhava in a few ways. The way that is most well-known nowadays is the one that went from - Longchen Rabjam and from there to Jigmey Lingpa. Because it came through Longchen Rabjam it is called "Longchenpa's Nyingthig" and that is usually abbreviated to "Longchen Nyingthig".

Jigmey Lingpa had three main disciples, one of whom was Jigmey Gyalwa'i Nyugu. One of his important disciples was Dza Patrul [1808-1887]. Dza Patrul wrote several texts on Longchen Nyingthig practice while living at Dzogchen monastery, including a text for his disciples that summed up the meaning of Garab Dorje's "The Three Lines that Strike the Key Points" teaching. This text became very famous and today is one of the most widely-used texts for explaining Thorough Cut practice. Dza Patrul's text is titled *Feature of the Expert Glorious King* though many know it as "The Three Lines that Strike the Key Points" because of the teaching contained in it.

Feature of the Expert Glorious King is very short and good for memorization but does need explanation. Dza Patrul wrote a short commentary to the text which is usually published together with it. Padma Karpo Translation Committee has published a book containing a translation of the text and its commentary[3] as well as the Tibetan texts. A few other commentaries to the text have been written though most are very short.

Dza Patrul stayed for many years at Dzogchen Monastery where he planted the teaching of Longchen Nyingthig very strongly. The lineage passed from him down through several Dzogchen Monastery lineage masters until in the mid-twentieth century it was received by Lodro Gyatso, who became a great yogin and eventually a buddha in the mountain retreats of Dzogchen monastery.

Lodro Gyatso gave the Longchen Nyingthig teaching, including the Three Lines teaching and Dza Patrul's *Feature of the Expert Glorious King* teaching, to many disciples. One of his closest disciples, Ontrul Tenpa'i Wangchuk, wrote a detailed commentary to *Feature of the Expert Glorious King* which has been translated and presented in this book.

Lodro Gyatso and Ontrul Tenpa'i Wangchuk

Lodro Gyatso of Dzogchen Monastery lived during the twentieth century and was one of the greatest Dzogchen practitioners in Tibet in recent times. He stayed in retreat in the mountains, gained the realization of Great Completion, and in doing so kept the practice tradition alive despite the calamities that accompanied the Communist Chinese

[3] *Feature of the Expert Glorious King*, by Tony Duff, second edition, published by Padma Karpo Translation Committee, December 2008, ISBN: 978-9937-8244-3-9.

invasion. He was one of the very important few who maintained the continuity of realization and practice between the situations before this disaster in Tibet and afterwards. At the time of his death in 2003, the seven signs of a manifest buddha appeared—the same signs that appeared when Longchen Rabjam attained enlightenment—and he was understood to be someone who attained buddhahood in his lifetime through the profound practices discussed in this book. He became very famous for the power of his practice and realization and his memory is cherished today.

At the time of the Communist Chinese invasion, Lodro Gyatso and Ontrul Tenpa'i Wangchuk were gaoled and put in the same cell where they stayed together for seventeen years. Lodro Gyatso passed his entire lineage to Tenpa'i Wangchuk during that time and Tenpa'i Wangchuk developed great mastery and scholarship because of it. After their release, they went to their respective places in East Tibet where each did what he could to maintain the Buddhist teaching and cause it to flourish again.

Lodro Gyatso has passed into nirvana but Tenpa'i Wangchuk is still alive at the time of writing. In his early 70's, he is regarded as the most learned of the Dzogchen masters in Tibet not to mention one of the most realized.

In recent years, Tenpa'i Wangchuk has written a series of commentaries on important subjects of Great Completion. His writings are known for having an unusual clarity. For example, his commentary on Longchen Rabjam's all-important *Dharmadhatu Treasury*, which is the only commentary ever written on this key text except for Longchenpa's own commentary, is exceptionally clear, settling many points that cannot be settled using Longchenpa's own commentary.

Tenpa'i Wangchuk's commentaries come from high realization and have been written in our own time. These two factors mean that the blessings associated with them are very strong. Moreover, they are a direct conduit to the extraordinary level of realization of his guru Lodro Gyatso who also is very close to us in time. Altogether, the level of blessings available through these commentaries is very high, which is an exceptionally important point for anyone who is practising this material.

"Relics of Dharmakaya"

Ontrul Tenpa'i Wangchuk composed his *Relics of Dharmakaya* commentary to Dza Patrul's *Feature of the Expert Glorious King* by rounding up his notes on teachings that he had received from Lodro Gyatso, then compiling them into one text. The commentary goes through Dza Patrul's *Feature of the Expert Glorious King* from beginning to end, commenting on every word of the text as it goes.

Dza Patrul writes in the conclusion to the *Feature of the Expert Glorious King* that the Three Lines teaching contained in the text is an ultimate teaching that came out of his own, ultimate space of realization.

> "Rigpa's liveliness, the dharmakaya treasure
> revealer,
> Takes the treasure from the space of prajna ..."

Ontrul Tenpa'i Wangchuk, Golok, 2007.

Guru Rinpoche and his manifestations.
Mural on the wall of Dzogchen Monastery,
Tibet, 2007. Photograph by the author.

I have heard in person from practitioners who were direct disciples of Lodro Gyatso, that he was a person of ultimate attainment and that, when he taught, it had this same kind of quality to it. Tenpa'i Wangchuk received the teachings contained in *Relics of Dharmakaya* from Lodro Gyatso in the ultimate way. Therefore, I strongly suspect that the name "Relics of Dharmakaya" was not intended just as a nice piece of wording but is a deliberate reference to this text as being a pearl of his guru's own realization of dharmakaya. Either way, this commentary is for us a pearl of Lodro Gyatso's personal realization and the power of his lineage. It does have a very strong connection to dharmakaya, which is one of the things that makes it an outstanding commentary on Dza Patrul's text. This is an important point, because texts like this are about something that is actually transmitted by blessings, not by words on a page.

Relics of Dharmakaya is, in general, very clearly written. Moreover, it has the feature that it clarifies the meaning of *Feature of the Expert Glorious King* word by word. On top of that, it has the blessings of an author who possessed the direct lineage of Dza Patrul's teaching. Above all, it is filled with the special blessings of Lodro Gyatso and his ultimate transmission of the teaching to the author. For all of these reasons, it is considered to be the best commentary ever written to Dza Patrul's text.

Relics of Dharmakaya proceeds through *Feature of the Expert Glorious King* from beginning to end, quoting a piece then commenting on it as it goes. During the translation of *Relics*, we obtained the text for these quotes from our translation of the *Feature* mentioned above. However, we went a step further. The Tibetan wording of the *Feature*, its commentary, and this commentary is the same in many places, so we went through the translations of all three to ensure that their vocabfsulary and wording matched as well. It is unusual to find Tibetan texts that have been matched for consistency of translation like this and I am particularly pleased to be able to present this kind of forward-looking work. It has the very desirable effect for the reader that the meaning in these texts becomes as accessible and useful as it is in the Tibetan originals.

Revealed Treasure Marks

Tibetan writing uses a specific punctuation mark to show breaks. The usual form is simply a vertical stroke. However, that is replaced in revealed treasure texts with a variant called a "revealed treasure mark" which looks like this ༔ . During the 1980's the Nalanda Translation Committee was translating revealed treasures and discussed their work with Dilgo Khyentse Rinpoche who was visiting at the time. He said that it was important to retain the revealed treasure marks because they immediately and definitely indicate to the reader that the text is revealed treasure. Accordingly, all revealed treasure marks are shown in the translation.

About Sanskrit

Sanskrit terminology is properly transliterated into English with the use of diacritical marks. These marks often cause discomfort to less scholarly readers and can distance them from the work. This work, although it deals with Thorough Cut with great precision, is mainly for the use of practitioners, so diacritical marks have not been used in the translation.

Study

Padma Karpo Translation Committee has amassed a wide range of materials to help those who are studying this and related topics. Please see the chapter "Supports for Study" at the end of the book for the details.

Health Warning

The commentary here is about a subject that is normally kept secret; the concluding lines of the *Feature of the Expert Glorious King* make this very clear. Therefore, I have translated the commentary as it is, providing enough notes so that someone who does understand the meaning could understand the translation without mistake. However, I have deliberately not given any further explanation of or commentary to the meaning. Anyone who has had these teachings in person will be able to understand them or at least go to his teacher and ask for an explanation. Anyone who has heard these teachings in person from a qualified teacher, and especially who has had the introduction to the nature of mind[4] around which the teachings hinge, please use and enjoy the text as you will. However, if you have not heard these teachings and if you have not had a proper introduction to the nature of your mind, you would be better off not reading this book but seeking out someone who could teach it to you.

---

[4] Introduction to the nature of mind is often mistakenly called "pointing-out instruction". For "introduction", see the glossary.

In short, the contents of this book could be dangerous to your spiritual health if you are not ready for it, so exercise care! I have many times in the last few years run into young students who are extremely confident of their understanding of the meaning of these profound systems but who just spout words that they have obtained from books. The solidity of their minds is noticeable.

PHAT cuts the elaboration,
HUM HUM HUM is the song of the dharmakaya arrived at,
PHEM PHEM PHEM is the warmth of the empty space,
HO HO HO is the jolly warrior giving you the goods.

Lama Tony Duff,
Swayambhunath,
Nepal,
May 2010

"RELICS OF DHARMAKAYA"

NOTES ON THE THREE LINES THAT STRIKE THE KEY POINTS COMPILED FROM THE WORDS OF MY GLORIOUS HOLY GURU

by Ontrul Tenpa'i Wangchuk

This compilation of notes on *The Feature of the Expert Glorious King* concerning the teaching called "The Three Lines that Strike the Key Points" has three parts of prefatory material, main text, and conclusion that correspond to its being good in the beginning, good in the middle, and good at the end[5].

---

[5] The Buddha once explained that dharma is always good. He said that it is "good in the beginning, good in the middle, and good at the end". A tradition then grew up of explaining dharma by separating it into prefatory, main, and concluding parts, which were joined to the dharma's goodness in the beginning, middle, and end respectively.

1. Prefatory Material

The *Three Lines* says[6],

Homage to the guru.

Of the three systems associated with Great Completion's method for introducing rigpa—the system of view acquired through hearing and contemplation, the system of meditation acquired through foremost instruction[7], and the system of transmission of blessings—the presentation here follows the last one. For that method of introducing rigpa, a disciple takes the four empowerments with a mixture of intense faith, devotion, and trust that comes from understanding that the guru is an embodiment of the buddhas of the three times. The disciple then mixes his mind with the guru's mind with the result that the realization of the guru's mindstream is transferred to his mindstream.

---

[6] Starting here, the author first cites Dza Patrul's one or more lines from the *Feature of the Expert Glorious King* then comments on them, word by word. In this translation, the cited lines are shown in plain italics. Following that, the individual words as they are commented on are highlighted using bold italics.

Note that, although the title of Dza Patrul's text is *Feature of the Expert Glorious King*, it is commonly known by the words of the teaching it expounds, Garab Dorje's "Three Lines that Strike the Key Points". Thus, *Three Lines* here and elsewhere in the text is a reference to Dza Patrul's *Feature* text.

[7] For foremost instruction, see the glossary.

No matter how swift-acting the compassionate activity and blessings of the buddhas might be, unless the disciple has in his own time a spiritual friend upon whom he can rely as a guru, there can be no way to realize the profound foremost instructions of Great Completion.

There are two gurus. The spiritual friend who shows the meaning to the disciple is called the simile guru. Appearing in the form of a person with body, face, and limbs, the simile guru bestows empowerment, explains tantra, and gives the foremost instructions but, most importantly, shows, naked and uncontrived, the superfactual bodhicitta wisdom[8] that is innate to and primordially present in the disciple. Accordingly, a spiritual friend who does this is called the guru of the three kindnesses. Dza Patrul prostrates and so pays ***homage to*** that kind of ***guru***. Then there is also the guru which is what is shown to the disciple; called the factual guru, it is the dharmata luminosity-wisdom seated at the centre of the disciple's heart. When, through the use of the simile guru's foremost instructions, this guru is woken up, it becomes the unborn factual guru and, after that, whenever the disciple manifests then cultivates it, that itself is the best of homages, the one called "the homage of meeting the view".[9]

---

[8] For superfactual bodhicitta wisdom, see the glossary. This terminology echoes Longchenpa's explanations in his *Dharmadhatu Treasury*, as clearly explained in Tenpa'i Wangchuk's commentary on the first chapter of that treasury. Thus, the term here does not mean path bodhicitta but primordial superfactual mind of enlightenment.

[9] In the Vajra Vehicle teachings, a guru in general has three (continued...)

2. Main Text

This has two parts: a synopsis and an explanation.

2.1 Synopsis

This has two parts: the actual subject and ancillary teaching on the benefits of being a fortunate person.

2.1.1 Actual Subject

The *Three Lines* says,

> *The view is Longchen Rabjam;*
> *The meditation is Khyentse Ozer;*
> *The conduct is Gyalwa'i Nyugu.*

Generally speaking, a person who follows the short path of Luminosity Great Completion[10] is using a method for going

---

[9](...continued)
kindnesses—he bestows empowerment, explains the tantras, and gives the foremost instructions. More important again is the guru who gives the introduction to mindness (see the glossary) in such a way that mindness is seen nakedly, clearly, just as it is. That guru is called the simile guru because he is not the factual guru but is something like it. One can pay homage to both types of guru. In the text, Dza Patrul is paying homage to the simile guru. Homage to the factual guru happens when a practitioner is actually meeting the factual guru in the factual view.

[10] Great Completion practice focusses on the nature characteristic of the three characteristics of mindness, which is luminosity.
(continued...)

to buddhahood in one life and in this body[11] in which threefold view, meditation, and conduct are kept as an unseparated whole for the purpose of manifesting the ultimate fruition. Because of that, Patrul's explanation in the *Three Lines* is given on the basis of joining threefold view, meditation, and conduct to the meaning of the names of three of his close lineage gurus.

When Patrul's text says "***the view***" how should that be understood? In this context, the view ***is*** a ***space***[12] that is a single unique sphere of empty knowing[13], a ***great***[14] expanse

---

[10](...continued)
Therefore, Great Completion is called Nature Great Completion and also Luminosity Great Completion. The name does not mean that Great Completion is luminous.

[11] This is the way in these teachings of saying "in one life and in this very life".

[12] Tib. klong. "Space" is the first part of Longchen Rabjam's name.

[13] Tib. stong rig. Empty knowing is actually the dynamic sense of "being empty and rigpa'ing" where both empty and rigpa are being used as verbs. Note that the placement first of "empty" tells us that being empty is being emphasized. Note that the reverse formulation can be and is used, in which case the knowing quality, the rigpa, is being emphasized. Pairs like this are used throughout the text and one should be attuned to the way in which the first member of the pair is, usually, the more important member in the context of the discussion.

[14] Tib. chen. "Great" is the next part of Longchen Rabjam's name.

that at once includes and wholly comprehends[15] all the dharmas of samsara and nirvana. And, these ***boundless universes***[16] of the appearances of samsara and nirvana which are shining forth[17] from the liveliness[18] of the great expanse of such view, shine forth without unstopped, evident and unmixed, yet, as they shine forth, all of samsara and nirvana never wavers from the expanse of rigpa-dharmata, great equality.

Precisely that undertaken as a practice is "***meditation***" so, when the text says meditation, how should that be understood? It has to be ascertained as the unifying of two things—the ***knowledge***[19] of unmistakenly knowing the fact just exactly as it is of the actuality of all dharmas—superfactual bodhicitta great dharmakaya's fact, and the ***love***[20] of great compassion that arises without conceived effort for the

---

[15] "At once includes and comprehends" is a standard phrase used in these teachings. It means that the single unique sphere that is empty and knowing both includes and knows at the very same moment all of the dharmas of samsara and nirvana.

[16] Tib. rab 'byams. "Boundless universe(s)" is the next part of Longchen Rabjam's name. It can be singular or plural. If singular it means the single unique sphere. If plural it means the limitless universes of samsara and nirvana which make up the single unique sphere.

[17] For shine forth and its variants see the glossary.

[18] For liveliness, see the glossary.

[19] Tib. mkhyen. "Knowledge" is the first part of Khyentse Ozer's name.

[20] Tib. brtse. "Love" is the second part of Khyentse Ozer's name.

sentient beings who have not realized such. Therefore, given that the wisdom that knows the fact as it is as just described—vipashyana that distinctly sees[21] the face of rigpa—is equivalent to the sun[22], and given that the non-referential great compassion of love that wholly sees migrators as many as they are is equivalent to the sun's ***light rays***[23], a meditation that unifies the two is referred to with "the meditation is Khyentse Ozer".

Then, what is the ***conduct*** of view, meditation, and conduct where the three are kept as an unseparated whole? The *Three Lines* says, "The conduct is Gyalwa'i Nyugu", which is a metaphor. A sprout gives rise to something very large with trunk, leaves, fruit, and so on. In relation to that, if the ***conquerors'***[24] sons with ***sprout***[25]-like bodhicitta train in the path of the simile six pāramitās[26], then the dharmas that are

---

[21] This is a nice play on words that shows the meaning of vipashyana. Vipashyana is translated into Tibetan with lhag thong. Distinctly here is "lhag ger" and sees is "mthong".

[22] This is one of the main examples of rigpa explained in Longchenpa's *Dharmadhatu Treasury*.

[23] Tib. 'od zer. "Light rays" is the last part of Khyentse Ozer's name.

[24] Tib. rgyal ba'i. "Conquerors'" is the first part of Gyalwa'i Nyugu's name.

[25] Tib. myu gu. "Sprouts" is the last part of Gyalwa'i Nyugu's name.

[26] Simile here has the same meaning as simile in "simile guru" and "simile wisdom", both of which are used in this text. In this case, it means that these are not the factual paramitas but (continued...)

the fruitions of enlightenment—the four kayas, the five wisdoms, and so on—will arise like trunks and leaves in a self-arising, conceptual-effort-less, spontaneously-coming-into-existence, manner.

Generally, there ***is*** in equipoise's rigpa a great accumulation, a primordially Great Completion and, because of that, all the qualities of the six paramitas are inherently complete in it[27]; the generosity of not grasping at anything, the discipline of having no attachment to anything, the patience of not being scared of anything, the perseverance involving no conceived effort, the absorption which is rigpa's abiding in itself of itself, and the prajna which is the self-arising prajna of rigpa are complete in the practitioner. The force of that causes the six paramitas to arise of themselves in post-attainment—the time of doing the activities of the conduct. Therefore, all the conduct of the conqueror's sprouts, meaning the bodhisatvas[28], is assistant to the great rigpa wisdom.

That is one way of connecting to the meaning of view, meditation, and conduct, though there are others, too. In the notes of Yukhog Chadralwa[29], a way of joining them to

---

[26](...continued)
something similar to them.

[27] This point is one of the topics of *Dharmadhatu Treasury*.

[28] This is the correct spelling of bodhisatva according to the Tibetan tradition. It has been so since the great translations done in the 9th century C.E.

[29] Yukhog Chadralwa [1872-1952] was a disciple of Adzom Drukpa; see *A Marvelous Garland of Rare Gems* by Nyoshul
(continued...)

the names of the gurus of the three lineages is seen: the conqueror's mind lineage connects with Longchen Rabjam; the vidyadhara's sign lineage with Jigmey Lingpa[30], and the person's aural lineage with Gyalwa'i Nyugu. Furthermore, and in accordance with the way that my holy guru spoke about it, the three gurus can be joined to view, meditation, and conduct to highlight that each one's particular feature. For example, with view, mentioning someone like Garab Dorje in the Noble Land and someone like Longchen Rabjam in Tibet speaks of the very pinnacle of all views. For meditation, mentioning someone like Jigmey Lingpa, whose meditation without fail day and night resulted in prajna born of meditation pouring forth so that, even though he had not trained in the five areas of knowledge, he had unhindered knowledge of all them, features his equipoise. For conduct, mentioning someone like Dza Trama Lama[31], would be to talk about someone who, not being stained by the slightest downfall due to improper conduct, was an example of having gone to the far shore of the conduct of the conquerors' sons.

---

[29](...continued)
Khenpo, translated by Richard Barron, and published by Padma Publishing. His writings have become very popular amongst Longchen Nyingthig followers these days because he accumulated a vast amount of Longchen Nyingthig teaching and developed high realization to go with it.

[30] Jigmey Lingpa was also known as Khyentse Ozer.

[31] Dza Trama was the common name of Jigmey Gyalwa'i Nyugu. He was famous for his perfect observance of the bodhisatva's conduct.

2.1.2 Ancillary Teaching on the Benefits of Being A Fortunate Person

The *Three Lines* says,

> *When you practise like that,*
> *Buddhahood in one life presents no difficulty*
> *And if not, still rational mind is happy* **A LA LA.**

When a person mentally casts aside all worldly affairs for the rest of this life and keeps to isolated mountain areas, doing one-pointed ***practice*** of the three things of view, meditation, and conduct all kept as an unseparated whole ***like that***, if he is a person with the fortune of karmic connection that gives him the highest perseverance and the highest faith, then his being liberated right over the alpha purity ground and going to ***buddhahood in*** this ***one*** human ***life will present no difficulty***.

However, we of this time of degeneration have little faith and devotion, our compassion is small, and our diligence and determination are weak, so it is difficult to guarantee that we will definitely complete the practise of this dharma and be liberated in this life. ***And*** "If not, still rational mind is happy A LA LA" means that, even ***if*** that does ***not*** happen, ***still*** for the yogin who practises this dharma, his ***rational mind***[32] being in a spacious and ***happy*** state, he knows how to bring whatever appears in this life to the path. Because of that, he has no clinging and attachment to confused appearances now and decides that samsara is useless and

[32] For rational mind, see the glossary.

future lives are futile, with the result that he has no desire for anything less than staying in a nature nirmanakaya field of one kind or another[33]. Therefore, the text says "***A LA LA***", to arouse delight at the prospect of practising this type of foremost instruction.

2.2 Explanation

Of view, meditation, and conduct, view will be explained first. View has three parts: introduction to oneself, decision on one thing, and assurance of liberation.

2.2.1 Introduction to Oneself

The *Three Lines* says,

> *For the view, Longchen Rabjam,*
> *The three line's meanings strike their key points.*
> *First, put your mind into a relaxed state.*
> *Not elaborating, not concentrating, be without discursive thought.*
> *In that state, when there is an even dwelling of the relaxation,*
> *Exclaim a sudden rational-mind striking PHAṬ,*
> *Its force delivered sharp and short, E MA HO!*
> *Nothing whatsoever, blankness;*
> *In the blankness, a transparency of view;*
> *The transparency viewed is inexpressible;*
> *Identify the dharmakaya rigpa!*
> *Introduction to oneself; that is the first key point.*

---

[33] It is part of the Nyingthig teaching that a person who cannot manage enlightenment in this life will aim for enlightenment in the dharmata bardo or at very least in the field of a nirmanakaya buddha, one based on the nature, luminosity.

The text says, "***For the view, Longchen Rabjam,***" which is like this. ***The three lines*** are introduction to oneself, decision on one thing, and assurance built on liberation; utilizing the oral instructions that contain their ***meanings*** to ***strike their key points***, cuts the artery of confusion. For example, just as a slaughterer who is expert at the key points of killing is able to kill whatever is to be slaughtered so that it dies immediately, someone who is expert at the foremost instructions aimed at striking the key points of the three lines' meanings is able to kill samsara with its confused appearances so that it dies immediately.

What does "introduction to oneself" mean? To begin with, there is a method for introducing the view when it has not yet been introduced. In the Vehicle of Characteristics, the view is determined using authoritative statement and reasoning; for authoritative statement, the Conqueror's words and the treatises[34] that support it are used and for reasoning, the seven chariots[35] and reasonings such as the five-fold reasoning—existence and non-existence in production and cessation, production and cessation in the four extremes, the Vajra Slivers, the reasoning of separation from one and

---

[34] "Authoritative statement" refers to both the speech and recorded words of the Buddha and of his followers who have accurately presented his dharma. "The Conqueror's words" are the recorded words of the Buddha, as preserved in the *Translated Word*, the *Kangyur*. "The treatises" are the texts written by his followers as preserved in the *Translated Treatises*, the *Tangyur*.

[35] The Seven Chariots is the name of a set of seven reasonings that dissect a chariot to arrive at emptiness. It was taught by Chandrakirti in his *Entering the Middle Way*.

many, and so on—are used[36]. There are many ways of determining the view in the ordinary system of Secret Mantra, such as by using the simile wisdom of the three empowerments then using the fourth empowerment to introduce factual wisdom. However, we are discussing the extraordinary system here. Thus, when the view is determined using its particular approach, that of the most secret, unsurpassed Great Completion[37], the following is done.

First, the body is set relaxed, motionless like a mountain, with the legs crossed up, the two hands put in the mudra of resting up in mindness[38], the spine held straight, and the eyes staring into space. That is the method for placement

---

[36] The Middle Way school called the Consequentialist Middle Way uses five main reasonings to arrive at emptiness, four of which have been mentioned here by name.

[37] The are three main levels of Dzogchen teaching. In order of increasing profundity they are: mind section, space section, and foremost instruction section. The last of the three has been further divided into three and also into four subsections of increasing profundity, with the most profound of them named "most secret". That one has also been named the "innermost" in relation to all of the other levels. It has also been named "unsurpassed" given that it is the highest level of all of these levels. These names are used in Great Completion teaching to indicate the level of the teaching under discussion.

[38] Tib. sems nyid ngal gso. This is the mudra where the palms of the hands are placed over the knees. For mindness, see the glossary.

of the body. The Nyingthig hearing lineage's *Profound Scroll* says[39],

> "If the body is straight, the channels are straight. If the channels are straight, the winds are straight. If the winds are straight, you have the purpose of it, which is a workable mind."

Similar to that, the wind of speech must be left natural, with breathing being done gently through the mouth, because wisdom winds move via the mouth and impure winds move via the nose. When that it done, it causes the wind inside the Kati Crystal Tube to move in a balanced way and, when that happens, the twenty-one thousand winds cease in their own place and the purpose is accomplished, which is that the confused appearances coming from the mass of thoughts are pacified of themselves. The *View, Cloudless Sky*[40] says,

> "The breath is done as inhalation and exhalation
> through the teeth,
> A key point of the Kati Crystal Tube
> connecting from heart to mouth.

---

[39] There is a hearing lineage associated with the Dakini Nyingthig teachings from Padmasambhava that came through Longchenpa. It is a threefold set called the Nyingthig Hearing Lineage Trilogy. It is several times mentioned in this text simply as "the hearing lineage".

[40] This is a text written by Tenpa'i Wangchuk's root guru Lodro Gyatso. It has become famous nowadays in East Tibet. It is a short text about Thorough Cut with a companion text about Direct Crossing, There is a very long commentary to it by Tenpa'i Wangchuk which we hope to translate in the future.

When, by this key point the karmic winds have stopped, the mass of thought is pacified and
Thorough Cut's view, which is self-outputting[41], shines forth directly.
It is a foremost instruction for making rigpa manifest."

and Drubwang Zhabkar[42] said,

"The key point of wind is not to send it through the nose but through the mouth;
With both teeth and lips held not quite touching
The wind is breathed extremely gently in and out."

and the hearing lineage[43] says,

"The wind of the speech, natural, without conceptual effort, is sent out a little longer from the mouth. By doing that, the coming and going of karmic wind is put in its own place whereby the winds of afflictions—which are nothing but thought—dissolve of themselves and then rigpa, wisdom wind, swells throughout the expanse, which is this path's special feature."

That is the method for placement of the speech.

---

[41] Tib. gdangs. For output see the glossary.

[42] Tsele Natshog Rangdrol, also known as Zhabkar, was one of the great Great Completion practitioners of the nineteenth century. His teachings are well known.

[43] … of Longchen Nyingthig …

Similarly, mind should have no movement, no thinking, no meditation, no construction or alteration, no rejection or adoption, no suppression or furtherance done within it whatsoever. Rather, from the ***first*** you have to ***put your mind into a relaxed state***; you have to put it so that it is in its own place, which is a space-like state. If leaving it like that does not make these wild, coarse discursive thoughts of mind disappear, mindness's own face will not be seen, so this leaving yourself in a state divorced from the coarse, confused thought of the three times, relaxed and not thinking anything at all, is the method for placement of the mind.

The Adzom Drukpa camp puts the disciples to work on this for a period of four to five years[44]. And guru Mipham said[45]:

> "This is it! It might be causal alaya, nevertheless,
> if you do not do it this way, authentic wisdom
> will not be born in your mindstream.[46]"

meaning that this is the method for placement of the mind! This method must be used and then, because of it, wisdom that is the result of the method can be realized.

---

[44] Adzom Drukpa [1842-1924] was one of the most famous Great Completion practitioners of recent times in Tibet. His dharma centre was called Adzom Gar, meaning Adzom's Camp. It was, like many others in the area, an encampment with buildings for the shrine room and a few long-term residents.

[45] Mipham in this text is always in reference to Ju Mipham Namgyal.

[46] "Causal alaya" means that, at this stage of practice, one is still resting in a dualistic mind. Later, one will get to the main practice of indeterminate alaya. For alaya, see the glossary.

What the gurus of Great Completion's three lineages[47] assert about this is that all movement of mind—discursive thought—first has to vanish into its own place and then it is from there that introduction happens. Thus, no matter which external object of the sixfold group—visual form, sound, smell, taste, or touch—shines forth[48], do ***not*** involve yourself in discursive thinking that is ***elaborating*** about what is over there, and, similarly, no matter which thought of the three or five poisons shines forth, do ***not*** involve yourself in the use of antidotes against it that will have you ***concentrating***[49] inwards on a reference point in here[50]. When through that you have relaxed, you then must put yourself into and ***be*** in an equipoise ***without discursive thought*** of the three times—no thought of the past because it has ceased, no thought of the future because it has not

---

[47] The three lineages are: conqueror's mind lineage, vidyadhara's sign lineage, and person's aural lineage.

[48] The sixfold group is the set of six sense consciousnesses which we humans have. The external objects of the sixfold group are the objects of the five physical senses, as listed.

[49] Tib. bsdu ba. One goes out towards the external objects with thoughts elaborated about them and one withdraws inwards towards afflictions because of attempting to apply an antidote to them. The word concentrating here does not mean concentration in the sense of practising one-pointedness in meditation, it means to have withdrawn inwards as opposed to having gone outwards. In other words, the instruction here is to not follow our usual approaches of either going out after objects or coming in to deal with thoughts.

[50] Over there and in here are the two poles of objects known dualistically.

been produced, and no discursive thinking in the present because it has vanished of itself—in a state which is uncontrived and left to be itself, then give rise to luminosity wisdom from that. There is the problem at the beginner's level that, even though the beginner attempts to be self-settled without this elaborating and concentrating that is related to discursive thoughts and then attempts to preserve the state[51] of the innate, that latter part only partially happens. Instead of becoming a state of the innate, it turns into something like abiding only, with the beginner not being able to remove the outer coverings of clinging to the temporary experiences of bliss, clarity, and no thought. Therefore, ***in that state***, ***when there is an even***, that is, a ***dwelling*** sort ***of*** condition that has come from ***the relaxation*** of the three doors, if it happens that the practitioner is unable to remove the outer coverings of clinging to temporary experience and the worn out rags of discursive thinking, then in order to get free of them, in order to strip them off so that rigpa is left standing there stark naked and fully unveiled in transparency, Patrul Rinpoche says that it is necessary to ***exclaim a sudden rational-mind striking***—or thunderbolt like—***PHAṬ***. And the sound of the PHAṬ should not be a pleasant one with melody and drawn out tune, rather, the PHAṬ must be exclaimed so that ***its*** sound has a strong ***force*** which is ***delivered sharp***[52] ***and short***.

The PHAṬ sound provides a condition that can strip away the coverings in their entirety of thoughts of the three times

---

[51] For preserve and state, see the glossary.

[52] Tib. ngar. Intense means a lot of force delivered in a very short time.

and clinging to temporary experiences, so that rigpa, your in-dwelling wisdom, is freed of them and nakedly revealed. Rigpa revealed that way is the rigpa factor of the birthless state fully unveiled, nakedly revealed, and un-stopped. It is wisdom freed from eightfold consciousness that is not something that was not present before that has been newly created but is the co-emergent wisdom beyond mind that never has been and never will be apart from you. Thus it is that, with nothing held back, you have been introduced to and met the ultimate mind of the buddhas of the three times, the heart's blood of hundreds of thousands of mother dakinis that is the quintessence of the eighty-four thousand-fold dharma heap. This is marvellous indeed so the text says, ***E MA HO!***

At this point, you are free of all identifications[53] such as "exists", "does not exist", "is", "is not", and so on, therefore it is called, "***nothing whatsoever***", and the liberation of

---

[53] Tib. ngo bzung. An identification is something that occurs only in conceptual mind. It refers to the process in which an object of the senses is identified by conceptual mind as being such and such, where such and such is a conceptual tag.

being free of all vacillatory foci[54] such as "it is this" having been manifested, it is called "***blankness***".

The introduction given at the time of empowerment is done this way, too. Six methods for giving introduction are stated in *Sound Breakthrough*[55] and this is one of them. The guru can exclaim the sound PHAṬ or you can exclaim a forceful PHAṬ at yourself, either is all right, then, when the mass of thoughts of the three times has been totally severed because of it, you look at the in-dwelling wisdom that has been made manifest, and that is it!

---

[54] Tib. gza' gtad. This term is twice pejorative. "Vacillatory" refers to a process of hovering around a subject, seeing it from this angle and that angle because of vacillating over how it really is. "Focus" means that rational mind takes one of the possible angles and settles on that. For example, in the process of resting in the essence of mind, there can be the fault of not leaving rational mind but staying within in it and thinking, "Yes, this is the essence of mind" or "No, this is not it. It is that". Each of those is a vacillatory focus. Any vacillatory focus implies that the practitioner has not left rational mind and so is not in rigpa.

[55] Tib. sgra thal 'gyur. This is the name of the root tantra of the seventeen tantras of the innermost unsurpassed Great Completion teaching. The name refers to the fact that the audible sounds of the samsaric realm can be broken through using specific practices explained in the tantra. By doing so, they cease to be sounds of samsara, becoming sounds of nirvāṇa instead.

In this context, ***the*** term "***blankness***" is used to refer to being freed of the foci of mind[56] and "transparency of view" is used to refer to being freed of veils[57]. There are no veils at all given that all things over there[58] have been defeated—but you must understand that saying so indicates that there is the presence in here of something which has the seven qualities of a vajra and which cannot be damaged by anything. Thus, "blankness" here is not being used to refer to a blankness of mind understood as a bare emptiness or a mentally determined emptiness, or to something like Hvashang's view[59]. Rather, it is understood to mean "***a transparency of view***", a term whose use specifically refers to wisdom beyond mind being manifested by nakedly baring the empty-luminous-stoppageless rigpa.

Rigpa has now come forth and this is described using the words "***the transparency*** is being ***viewed***". The rigpa having been fully unveiled, there is the transparency of its being

---

[56] Tib. sems kyi gtad so. Foci of mind are the concepts that dualistic rational mind focusses on during its operation. Having foci of mind is the same as having the process of identification mentioned above.

[57] Tib. zang thal. Transparency means direct sight of something that comes when anything that would interfere with the view is absent. It happens because the veils of mind such as elaborations, references, and foci have been removed.

[58] Tib. phar gyi dngos po. "Things" here specifically means conceived of things. "Over there" makes the point that these are things being known dualistically.

[59] Hvashang's view refers to a mere absence of mentation which is then mistakenly equated with wisdom.

freed of all of elaboration's extremes—same and different, permanent and impermanent, existent and non-existent, is and is not, birth and cessation, and so on; in other words, this factor of rigpa that is there, bared naked, is like a crystal ball. It ***is inexpressible,*** meaning that it cannot be expressed either verbally with words or with the concepts of thinking mind. Therefore, Rāhula's *Praise of the Mother*[60] says,

> "Prajnaparamita inexpressible by speech and
> thought,
> No birth, no cessation, space-like,
> The domain of individual self-knowing wisdom,
> I prostrate to the mother of the conquerors of
> the three times."

Following on from that, the text continues with, "When you have freed mind of thoughts of the three times and then brought forth and looked at the inner character of mind, ***identify***[61] that cleared-out, pure part of rigpa that has been freed of all edge and centre[62] as what is called ***"the dharmakaya rigpa"!***"

---

[60] The Buddha's son, the arhat Rahula, composed this very famous praise of the mother of all the conquerors, Prajnaparamita.

[61] "Identify" here is the same word in Tibetan as the identification described a little earlier as a conceptual process. In this case it is a less technical way of talking and means to pick out the rigpa dharmakaya for oneself in one's own direct experience.

[62] Tib. mtha' dbus. Free of the concepts of edge and centre, the dharmakaya is unending vastness that cannot be met with the concepts of rational mind. Free of edge and centre means that the dharmakaya is beyond the concepts of "dimensionality" and therefore is all-encompassing.

That has also been said like this:

"This present awareness having unstopped,
cleared-out rigpa[63] ༔
Exactly is Samantabhadra the prime
guardian[64]. ༔"

Just like that, what has been described here—placement of the three doors in uncontrived relaxation followed by stripping down to naked, cleared-out, cleaned-out[65] rigpa freed of the thoughts of the three times—is the essential point of hundreds of words about Great Completion and the central issue of the view of Thorough Cut. As Zhabkar said,

"The central issue of Thorough Cut's view
stated as
'Rigpa is stripped naked then its cleared-out
state is preserved'
Alone is the important key point.
It is the essential point of hundreds of words,
therefore,

---

[63] It is has become common to translate rigpa into English with awareness, which is a mistake. In Tibetan texts, there is a general term for awareness, "shes pa" and there is also the specific term "rigpa". From the foregoing teaching it should be clear that rigpa is not simply an awareness. This sentence clearly shows the difference between awareness and rigpa.

[64] Tib. gdod ma'i mgon po. Prime Guardian is the term for the deity before all other deities; it is usually Samantabhadra in Nyingma and Vajradhara in Kagyu.

[65] By stripping all concepts from the rigpa it becomes cleared out like airing a stale room and cleaned out like removing the dirt from anything.

Fortunate heart sons, know that!"

When like that, you nakedly realize, free from thought and expression, the self-knowing[66], self-illumining, self-aware factor that is present in mind, because it wholly pervades samsara and nirvana, it is the wisdom pervading all samsara and nirvana and is universal mind of the conquerors of the three times, the great dharmadhatu[67]. In regard to this, Langdro Lotsawa said,

"This experience not conceivable in mind,
Abiding as naked self-illumination, and
The pervader of all samsara and nirvana
Is the understanding of the conquerors of the
three times."

When that has happened, no matter what type of discursive thinking moves in your mind, it will remain empty while it moves, like space being fully present while a wind blows through it. Therefore, if you make a firm decision about this naked, fully-unveiled-into-transparency, empty mindness, there is nothing else than that; as Mipham Rinpoche said,

"At that time, like having looked at
Space fully present there, your own mind
While it moves is emptiness—

---

[66] The actual wording is "self-rigpa'ing", with rigpa being a verb. It reads well in the Tibetan, with the constant focus being on rigpa and its way of knowing—rigpa'ing—in the practice of this path of Thorough Cut.

[67] For dharmadhatu, see the glossary.

> You need the certainty of a firm decision on
> that."

Prior to this, you were controlled by the confusion of looking outwardly and were not able to see the fact of actuality. However, you are now looking inwardly and the empty mind of rigpa which, having been freed of three parts of four, freed of all edge and centre, is cleaned-out and naked, has been manifested, and that is called "dharmakaya rigpa"[68]. As Mipham said,

> "Compared to the hundreds of far away dharmas looked at over there
> The one mind dharma looked at over here is supreme.
> Oh little children who cherish looking over there,
> Today it would be appropriate to look over here!"

This sort of naked, cleaned-out, cleared-out, fully-unveiled-into-transparency rigpa that cannot be expressed verbally or conceptually is the great self-arising wisdom. All of the objects of the sixfold group that shine forth from its state are the play of this self-arising wisdom's liveliness and have

---

[68] Note that the ordering of the words also contains information. The fact of the empty aspect is being emphasized at this level of the teaching. Therefore, the empty aspect is mentioned ahead of the rigpa, or knowing, aspect.

to be understood as its ornamentation[69]; Lotsawa Vairochana[70] said,

> "Inexpressible rigpa of fully-unveiled-
>   transparency,
> Beyond thinking, purified of the stains of mind
> Is the entity of self-arising wisdom with
> Everything that appears shining forth as
>   dharmakaya's ornament."

Palgyi Yeshe[71] said,

> "Self-arising wisdom: beyond rational mind;
> Mindness; space without centre or fringe;
> Eightfold group's appearances freed of
>   identification[72];
> The process of self-arising understanding—this
>   is it exactly.[73]"

---

[69] This point of the play and ornamentation is another of the topics of *The Dharmadhatu Treasury*.

[70] The Vairochana who was one of the twenty-four main disciples of Padmasambhava.

[71] Another of the twenty-four main disciples of Padmasambhava.

[72] The eightfold group is eightfold samsaric consciousness. Samsaric consciousness operates using the process of conceptual identification as explained earlier.

[73] If you look carefully at this compact verse, you will see that he starts by saying "self-arising wisdom", moves on to pointing out that it is mindness, like space, beyond rational mind, and in doing so is pointing out the empty aspect, called the entity. From there, he points out that the entity has a nature, which is
(continued...)

He is saying this. Self-arising rigpa-wisdom is as follows: it is the suchness which is the actuality of mind beyond the objects of rational-minded thought with its dualistic clinging; it is the alpha pure wisdom—alpha pure because like space, it does not come into existence above, below, at the edge, centre or anywhere in between—which is free of elaboration, which is equality; therefore, if for any appearance of the eightfold group that shines forth in that state, the state of great self-shining-forth-self-liberation is preserved, that will be all that is needed; there is nothing other than that.

Furthermore, Jigmey Tennyi[74] said,

> "Here, what we are talking about when we say "meditation" is something that has no entity that could be identified yet, if you stay in its state without straying from it, all the while knowing an entity of luminous emptiness that cannot be expressed, that is it!"

---

[73](...continued)
the luminosity with its appearances. If you can stay in the state of the entity and simultaneously allow all possible appearances to appear, unmodified, left just as they are, then that process of non-dual mind, which is a self-arising process, is exactly that self-arising wisdom.

[74] The first Dodrupchen Jigmey Trinley Ozer was, with Jigmey Gyalwa'i Nyugu, one of the main disciples of Jigmey Lingpa. The third Dodrupchen, Jigmey Tennyi, was famous for his extensive writings that clarified many key points of Great Completion practice. He is quoted several times in this text, sometimes being referred to simply as "Tennyi".

And Mipham Rinpoche said,

> "When you are right in rigpa you look, so to speak, but there is nothing at all to see; you are not seeing, but luminosity is operating from the depths; you are distracted away to something, but its entity is unchanging; you are not distracted to something, but you are free of focal points. That sort of thing is what is needed."

Thus, this is not something to be understood in a merely theoretical way with hearing, contemplating, and logic. Rather, you have in your own experience naked, undressed rigpa—a pristine pure emptiness that is the birthlessness of mind being groundless and rootless yet with crystal clear illumination that goes on without stoppage, a crystal clearness that blips away in vastness—and except for that there is nothing else to identify at all. It is like what a spiritual song of experience says,

> "For all that shines forth, Thorough Cut's prajna sword
> Cuts directly to what has boiled up from mind resulting in
> Separation from the identification "It is that, it is not this".
> It seems to me that simply that is the entity to be preserved; isn't it so?"

The foregoing has discussed the first of the three lines striking the key points, to give an introduction to oneself. The meaning of this line is that, initially, it is important to have such an introduction to the view because, without it, there will be no way to use meditation to preserve a state of the view. Moreover, it makes the point that this rigpa is not to be found in some place other than yourself and that it does not come from creating something in your mindstream which was not there before. This rigpa is the co-emergent wisdom that exists in you, primordially inseparable from you, so an ***introduction to*** that, based on ***yourself is the first key point***[75].

2.2.2 Decision on One Thing

The *Three Lines* says,

> *After that, proliferation or dwelling, either one is fine.*
> *Anger or attachment, happiness or sadness,*
> *At all times and in every circumstance there is*
> *Recognition, the dharmakaya is identified, and*
> *The previously-known mother luminosity meets with the son.*
> *Stay in the state of the inexpressible rigpa factor.*
> *Dwelling, bliss, clarity, joy—destroy them again and again.*
> *Suddenly bring down the syllable of method and prajna.*
> *Equipoise and post-attainment are not different;*
> *Session and between session are not distinct;*
> *Remain continuously in the inseparable state.*
> *Nonetheless, until finality has been obtained,*
> *Abandon frivolity then cherish meditation.*

---

[75] The first line literally says, "an introduction made based on oneself". The meaning of that has been clarified here: you are the one receiving the introduction; the person making it can be you or someone else; and what is being introduced is present in yourself. In other words, you are being introduced to yourself.

Practice should be done in defined sessions.
At all times and in every circumstance,
Preserve shifting events solely of the dharmakaya.
Make a decision that there is nothing other than that.
Decision on one thing; that is the second key point.

Now, ***after that*** first key point has been accomplished, the time comes to meditate in order to gain experience. At this time, if when dwelling you can identify that as the dharmakaya's own face, and if when elaborating you can identify that as wisdom's own liveliness, then dwelling will be the state of rigpa and elaborating will be the state of rigpa, too, so whether there is ***proliferating or dwelling, either one will be fine***. Either way, if you know how to relax into the birthless state of empty rigpa, then, whether meditating or not, however you are, there will not be any becoming distracted to something else. As it says in the *All Creating King*[76],

> "If, for each and every movement in the
> mentating, thinking mind,
> Without moving away from the state of
> birthlessness
> You know it as meditation no matter what has
> been thought,
> Then, however you are while not meditating,
> you never move away from it."

When you have realized the meaning intended there, you will, without needing either to further abiding or to stop proliferation, never depart from a concentration which is a

---

[76] Tib. kun byed rgyal po. The name of the root tantra of the mind section teachings of Great Completion.

flow of staying in the state or of non-meditation. It is like what Zhabkar said,

> "Rather than being involved over there in the
> contrivances made by rational mind,
> What comes forth from the blessings of the
> root and lineage gurus,
> Over here, the view pure like space,
> Is, like the uninterrupted flow of a river,
> Continuously preserved with undistracted
> mindfulness,
> Which is called 'the concentration of a flow of
> non-meditation'."

Similarly, when you have identified this, then you have this, which is called "rigpa left naturally, great bliss, the absorption of un-meditated spontaneous existence" in the time of the present moment, like a great river. Having this, if you set yourself in equipoise on uncontrived rigpa, the rigpa has the ability to be illuminated by its own state or strength; it is as the *Actuality Treasury*[77] says,

> "Self-resting, great-bliss vajradhatu,
> The supreme absorption of un-meditated
> spontaneous existence,
> Perpetually exists; when you set yourself in
> uncontrived equipoise on that
> So that it is like the flow of a great river, the
> state illuminates itself."

---

[77] Tib. gnas lugs mdzod. One of Longchenpa's Seven Treasuries, it transmits the meaning of innermost Great Completion by examining the four special samayas of Thorough Cut.

When there is that kind of abiding, thoughts of ***anger or*** aggression could be produced on the basis of an object that displeases mind, thoughts of ***attachment*** could be produced on the basis of an object that pleases mind, or ***happiness*** of mind could come forth ***or*** else ***sadness***, suffering of mind; nonetheless, all discursive thought that shines forth has to be known as the play of rigpa, the dharmata's shifting events or, you can say, dharmata's liveliness. When you have understood that, the foremost instruction concerning the five poisons not being discarded but being present as the five wisdoms becomes important. Therefore, ***at all times and in every circumstance***, rather than falling under the control of ordinary-type thoughts within the zone of confusion, you are to ***recognize*** the single unique sphere of the elaboration-free empty rigpa that was introduced to you earlier by the guru and ***identify*** everything that shines forth only as ***the dharmakaya*** rigpa—and not as anything else[78].

---

[78] This is Tenpa'i Wangchuk's way of explaining it; it is slightly different from Dza Patrul's explanation of it in his commentary. Dza Patrul says that you should recognize everything that arises as the wisdom you were introduced to and then, having done so, the dharmakaya will have been apprehended, and so on. Here, Tenpa'i Wangchuk is emphasizing the two-step approach of beginners in which one first recognizes the empty aspect of rigpa and then knows whatever shines forth as the liveliness of the rigpa so that it is apprehended as the dharmakaya.

Note that the author is using the imperative form, which is one way that the *Feature* text could be read, given that the text is ambiguous at that level. It could be, "Anger or attachment, happiness or sadness, whatever occurs, you should at all times recognize (what you have been introduced to)! And then, having done so, you will have brought whatever has arisen into

(continued...)

In regard to this, all appearances of the objects of the sixfold group and all appearances of confused thoughts that shine forth must be left to be themselves without any attempts to reject or adopt them whatsoever. No matter which thoughts of the five poisons shine forth, do not look at them thinking, "This one, that one", nor follow after them, nor hit out at them the way that you would when using an antidote against them, rather, approach them without hope or fear, letting them go their own way in the same way as an older person watches the doings of a small child, all the while immovably staying in the state of rigpa dharmakaya.

Whatever discursive thoughts—afflictions, and so on—shine forth, when they are considered from their primordial situation, they are, with their space-like, empty entity that has been empty of every stain from the outset, the dharmakaya luminosity present in the ground or the ground rigpa, comparable to "the mother". When they are considered according to their current situation, they are the rigpa of the luminosity that was introduced by the guru, the path luminosity, comparable to "the son". It says in the *Heart's Blood Instruction*,

> "All dharmas' absence of nature is the dharmata mother,
> Knowing the absence of nature is the dharmata son."

When the practitioner sees, like this, the face of unified—where unified means absolutely indivisible—luminosity of

---

[78](...continued)
the meditative state and through that the dharmakaya will have been apprehended ...".

the ground which he is acquainted with from before and luminosity of the path, it is referred to as "mother and son luminosities having met". Accordingly, Patrul Rinpoche says "***the previously-known mother luminosity meets with the son***".

Whatever discursive thought shines forth based on the appearing objects of the sixfold group, etcetera[79], the disposition or entity of every bit of it is the great elaboration-free wisdom of equality, dharmakaya ground luminosity or dharmakaya wisdom present in the ground—so it is called "ground luminosity, the mother". And in relation to that, the current situation's factor of rigpa that is nakedly shining forth as the unveiled self-knowing[80] that was introduced by the guru is called "son luminosity". The merging into inseparability of these ground and path luminosities in an expanse which is free of edge and centre is called "meeting of mother and son luminosities".

Dudjom's way of talking about this in *Training Appearances* is similar[81]:

---

[79] Where etcetera means "or the eightfold group or whatever other classification of consciousness might be made".

[80] Here the actual words are self-rigpa'ing, with rigpa being a verb. It reads well in the Tibetan, with the constant focus being on rigpa and its way of knowing—rigpa'ing—in the practice of this path of Thorough Cut.

[81] In this text "Dudjom" always refers to Dudjom Jigdrel Yeshe Dorje.

Tib. snang sbyang. This is a famous text of Dudjom Jigdrel Yeshe Dorje that has often been used in the West for teaching

(continued...)

> "Path rigpa is small in extent, like the space inside a vase or a drop of water in a bowl. Ground rigpa is the great liberation from extremes, the pervasively spread, ever-present space that is the great version of it that is free of ground and root; the display of unveiled utter transparency without object; that which pervades all of samsara and nirvana.
>
> Following on from that, for the path rigpa smaller in extent and cramped like the space in a vase, just as smashing a vase with a hammer causes its internal space to merge with the outer space such that the two spaces become inseparable, so, the arrival of the rigpa of the path at the ground or the merging of path and ground rigpa, means that the ground's rigpa, which is the great liberation from extremes has been made manifest. A yogin who does that is called "a yogin of pervasively spread space"."

This quotation additionally clearly shows the way in which mother and son luminosities merge.

A further quotation from Dudjom shows the progressive stages of the merging of mother and son luminosities:

> "Similarly: first, the rigpa of having had the introduction is like the first part of the early

---

[81](...continued)
this subject to practitioners.

> dawn[82]; in the middle, the rigpa of having gained assurance, free from equipoise and post-attainment[83] is like the daybreak; and finally the rigpa of having gained liberation from extremes is like the sun shining."

Generally, the stages that gradual-type persons must go through are well known as: recognizing, training up, and gaining finality. However, following what Dodrupchen Jigmey Tennyi said,

> "There are two things: that to be meditated on which is the entity rigpa; and the doer of the meditation which is the compassionate rigpa. Thus, you must familiarize yourself with this doer of the meditation, the compassionate rigpa or, you can say, the liveliness of rigpa, and then,

---

[82] In Tibetan and Indian timing, the three hours prior to the actual rising of the sun are called the early dawn. That period is divided into three, one-hour periods and his description here follows the sequence of those three periods. The quality of the first hour is just that faint shift that happens in the very early hours of the day, when the night is still there but the possibility of the sun's dawning has been known.

[83] An advanced stage of practice occurs when assurance has arrived because of personally experiencing that one is capable of this level of practice. At this stage, rigpa is "on" a lot of the time for the practitioner, without distinction between meditation sessions and post-meditation sessions. This level is connected with the final phase of practice of the second of three lines and the beginning phase of the third of the three lines.

> based on that, you are escorted right to that to be meditated on, the entity rigpa.[84]"

The process can also be understood as a process of something becoming increasingly evident, as happens in the process of smelting, cutting, then polishing gold.

For the person of sharp faculties—the sudden type of person who hears and is liberated—just the introduction given by the guru causes mother and son luminosities to merge into inseparability with the result that all objects after that shine forth as dharmata, and view and meditation become a single, sufficient solution, and there is even the possibility of appearance and mind merging into inseparability—though that will depend on the individual. These points here come from the way it is discussed in Onpo Samdrup's camp[85].

Generally, mind's nature which has been there primordially as luminosity is called "ground luminosity" and that, when it has been woken up through the guru's foremost instructions, is called "path luminosity". The obscurations initially

---

[84] The entity—meaning the thing itself—rigpa is the emptiness aspect. The knowing aspect, which is where compassion and all the other good qualities of enlightenment dwell, is rigpa's luminosity aspect. At first one recognizes the empty aspect. Having done so, training is concerned with the luminosity aspect. Doing that training enforces the realization of the empty aspect as non-dual with the luminosity aspect through which one reaches finalization, the end of the journey. In other words, training is a process of training up the luminosity so that all of its good qualities become manifest.

[85] Onpo Samdrup was another, relatively recent Longchen Nyingthig master from East Tibet.

present are purified and, having been purified, the fruition becomes manifest which is called the "fruition luminosity".

Rigpa which is ***inexpressible*** by speech and thought, one's own face which is empty, luminous, and stoppageless, is made manifest. Then, to ***stay in the state of that*** naked ***rigpa factor*** while letting it be itself is the holy key point, the most cherished of key points.

In the case of a beginner, after the view has been introduced and when he is working on lengthening the continuity of the meditation, if he clings to the temporary experiences of ***dwelling, bliss, clarity, joy***, then his own face of rigpa will be obscured and, as a result, the outer coverings of the three temporary experiences will arrive. If they arrive, he must again manifest the innate character, rigpa, and again give birth to wisdom that does not think discursively. If he clings to the temporary experiences of abiding, bliss, clarity, and joy, his meditation deviates into confusion's path so he must destroy the three temporary experiences again and again, each time returning to and preserving his innate character, rigpa. If he preserves and does not lose the rigpa, then, no matter which temporary experiences of bliss, clarity, and no-thought occur, the concentrations that come on with the experiences themselves and, moreover, any that follow on from them, will act as assistants that will enhance rigpa and be a basis for the accomplishment of rigpa's three kayas.

The temporary experiences can lead to these: the entity, no-thought, empty temporary experience brings vastness like being in the centre of space; the nature, luminosity temporary experience brings an open state of mind, all-illuminating like the orbs of the sun and moon; the compassionate-activity, liberation[86] temporary experience brings self-shining-forth-self-liberation in which all that occurs is traceless. All of them become obvious within the matrix of the wisdom that is revealed when the face of rigpa is nakedly exposed. If that does not happen because mind instead clings to the experiences of bliss, clarity, and no thought, the beginner must take the approach of ***destroying them again and again*** which is like what has been said in these words,

> "A yogin's meditation is bettered by destroying;
> A mountain torrent is bettered by crashing
> down."

The text continues by answering the question, "How is the destroying done?" When temporary experiences of dwelling, bliss, and clarity shine forth and because of it the practitioner has the clinging that goes with taking great joy in them, having happiness about them, he must smash them with a forceful sound of PHAṬ. He must ***suddenly bring down***, as though it were a thunderbolt descending, a forcefully sounded ***syllable*** PHAṬ—the unification ***of*** the ***method*** letter PHA that draws together the blessings of all the conquerors ***and*** the ***prajna*** letter Ṭ that cuts—to obliterate the outer covering of clinging to temporary experience, and then he must preserve the state of the in-dwelling wisdom which has been manifested as the naked rigpa factor of inexpressible empty luminosity.

---

[86] The fundamental quality of compassionate activity is that it works to liberate sentient beings.

Next, the text says that equipoise and post-attainment are not distinct. In relation to this, generally, the dharmakaya wisdom present in the ground sits as the great elaboration-free equality in which the two aspects of the dharmata—its empty factor which is expanse and its rigpa factor which is the empty factor's stoppageless output—are unified so it has within it no distinction into the individual items called "equipoise and post-attainment"; this does not need discussion. The sudden-type person of sharp faculties has this sort of equipoise and post-attainment in which the two have become merged inseparably; for him, since what shines forth comes forth having the aspect of naked rigpa, it comes without distinction into equipoise and post-attainment. However, gradual-type persons like ourselves, whose situation is one of meditating based on the key points of the guru's foremost instructions and our own experience, are attempting to meditate without distraction from and at all times in the state of inexpressible rigpa fully unveiled into transparency, so the text teaches us that we must have a meditation in which ***equipoise and post-attainment are not*** two distinct things ***different*** from each other.

Next, it is not that you manifest rigpa then meditate on preserving its disposition during sessions but slip into distraction from rigpa between sessions at the time of the four types of conduct of going, staying, eating, lying down—as though rigpa is to be tossed aside at that time. Instead, your approach must be one of never being moved from the state only of rigpa so that ***session and between session are not*** made ***distinct***. In this vein, Dudjom said,

> "No thought, no meditation, no preservation, no distraction away, no keeping it alive ..."

and someone else said,

> "Never experiencing meditation and never
> experiencing separation,
> Not separated from the meaning of not-
> meditation."

To paraphrase those two quotes: "If the concentration of a continuous flow of non-meditation is produced in your mindstream, because it will not have a whisker of meditation done with conceptual activity associated with it, meditation will never be known, and because there will not be even a moment's distraction away from the state of what actually is, separation from that state will never be known, and that being so, it will never depart from the fact of the profound actuality in which there is nothing to be meditated on. Therefore there will be no separation from the meaning of not-meditation".

Gradual types like ourselves who have not found that kind of assurance must rely on mindfulness always. We must at all times and in every circumstance ***remain continuously in the state*** in which our own dharmakaya face of rigpa-emptiness has risen nakedly because the distinction of meditating and not-meditating has not been made, that is, because of being in the state of ***inseparability***.

There are also those of extremely sharp faculties. Nature Great Completion describes the way in which they are suitable vessels using its own path terminology as follows:

> They are a sudden type who is liberated upon hearing and their way is said to be "realization and

> liberation at the same time, like Indrabhuti"[87]. Immediately on being introduced, the objects that shine forth for them shine forth as the dharmata, view and meditation become a single sufficient solution, and the appearing mind is liberated over the ground. A person like this has no meditation to be done and no meditator of it, so he definitely has no need of meditation that works in that way.

Nonetheless, there are the ones other than that, the less fortunate gradual types who are in the situation of dependency[88] due to being under the control of other—where other is the discursive thought of confusion. They must meditate ***until*** they have ***attained finality*** in relation to rigpa. In regard to this, Jigmey Lingpa said,

> "You might have been introduced to rigpa but if
> you do not familiarize yourself with its state,

---

[87] King Indrabhuti was a lineage holder of the higher tantras of ancient India. He is famous for having this kind of realization because it allowed him to retain his kingdom and the world of sensory delights rather than running off to a cave and rejecting it all.

[88] In Buddhism, a person is either independent or dependent. A person who is independent has sense consciousnesses that are wisdom and hence are not controlled by external objects. A person who is dependent has dualistic sense consciousness; his consciousnesses are out of control and pulled about by sense objects. Dependency is the samsaric situation and independence the liberated one.

> You will be like a small child who at the battlefront is taken by the enemy, discursive thought."

and,

> "Meditation's not the main thing, familiarization is[89], and
> If familiarization becomes a space of one's own experience, that is supreme meditation."

and,

> "Without hearing, what knowledge will you have?
> Without knowledge, what meditation will you have?
> Without meditation, what liberation will you have?"

The extent to which finalization[90] has occurred is measured by dreams. As is said, "You are locked in by signs and

---

[89] This is an important distinction here. Meditation strictly stated is the act of cultivating something new whereas familiarization is the act of becoming increasingly familiar with what is already there. In this kind of text, meditation is sometimes used in the stricter sense but is also used, as in the next quotation, to mean practice in general, whether it is conceptual meditation or non-conceptual familiarization. If familiarization turns into a space of realization—with space here meaning an environment inhabited in one's own experience—then that is the best meditation.

[90] Finalization was mentioned earlier as one of the three phases of practice in the terminology of this system.

behaviour"[91]. If your place of meditation is also a place of ***frivolity*** and distraction, then, no matter how long you meditate, a special type of realization will not be possible. Thus, if you want to produce realization of the authentic[92] in your mindstream, understand that, for those who ***abandon*** the world, toss aside discursive thoughts, rely on isolation, protect their discipline, meditate on compassion, develop devotion, and train at removing their obscurations, there is no way that they will not have circumstances conducive to practice. Therefore, do that, and ***then***, with a strong mind of rock-like determination, cherish ***meditation*** above all.

Serious meditators never waver even once from being in rigpa. Therefore, for them, there is no difference between equipoise and post-attainment. They do not lose their assurance of the view when they are coursing in post-attainment and they never depart from the state of meditation. Thus they have the special quality of being able to mix their experienced wisdom with post-attainment conduct. If beginners like ourselves who do not have that sort of quality set our own times for meditation by defining sessions for it,

---

[91] The extent to which one has progressed on the path of familiarization is measured by dreams, as described in other places in the Nyingthig teaching. Therefore, one cannot get past, that is, one is locked in by, the signs of the progress on the path that come through dreams, and not only that but one is also locked in by one's conduct. If your conduct is appropriate it will lead to success in your meditation, if not, such as with staying in places where there is much distraction, your meditation will not be successful.

[92] Tib. yang dag. The authentic is a name for reality.

it is true that we will have only a pretence of keeping the two practices of equipoise and post-attainment not different. However, we have not yet attained finality—that is our condition—so we are not yet able to mix the wisdom of equipoise with post-attainment at the times when we are in post-attainment. This is what we get in return for having an equipoise which is not yet able to hold its own. Because of our condition, we must make equipoise the more important of the two, then work at ***practice in*** four or six, and so on, ***defined sessions***, or else, as has been said,

> "In short periods, many times like drips of water filling an empty house ༑"

In other words, you are to train by doing many sessions each day. That is how your meditation ***should be done***.

If you do not do that, you might exert yourself at the regular practise of taking conduct onto the path but, for the most part, it will just come out as points of deviation that come from getting lost in your usual habits. In regard to this, one beginner said, "I do my equipoise in defined sessions then, at the time of coursing in post-attainment, as long as I simply do not forget it, that's good!" but Khenchen Jigmey Phuntshog[93] said in reply, "That sort of thing is very dangerous!" Thus, it is very important ***at all times and in every circumstance*** to do the practice of equipoise in defined sessions and then to mix post-attainment conduct with that, and very important that, overall, the state should be preserved continuously.

---

[93] The famous guru of Serta who died just after the turn of the second millennium. Tenpa'i Wangchuk was a student of his, too.

If you do not preserve the state like that, then it could happen when you are practising equipoise that you are just believing in what you are doing conceptually. Then, when you attempt to mix that with conducting yourself in post-attainment, because you have not learned how to preserve the continuity of the equipoise state, you can fall under the control of discursive thought, lose your three doors to being ordinary ones, and there will be no benefit at all.

Thus, it is important at the time of post-attainment with its four types of conduct, to preserve the transparency of view of the subsequent consciousness[94]. Until you have produced the wisdom of inseparable equipoise and post-attainment, there will be two phases—equipoise and post-attainment. And for you, as a beginner, each phase will have to be separately known and dealt with as such: in the equipoise phase, the face of rigpa is to be preserved and in the post-attainment phase, that face is to be preserved by remembering it again and again. In regard to the ordinary person, Khenchen Jigmey Phuntshog Rinpoche has said that, "Seeing the face of rigpa, just as it is, in post-attainment is difficult compared to simply setting oneself into mindfulness in post-attainment."

Having understood that there is no discarding of so-called "desire, aggression, and delusion" to be done and there is no adopting of so-called "loving kindness, compassion, and bodhicitta" to be done, you make the decision that there is

---

[94] Tib. rjes shes. This refers to the sense consciousnesses at the time of post-attainment. The practitioner has to be able mix them with rigpa that was trained up in formal sessions of equipoise.

nothing else to be meditated on apart from preserving the view of rigpa. You decide that your practice, whenever and whatever, will be one of ***preserving*** all that happens as the ***shifting events solely*** of the view ***of the*** great rigpa-empty ***dharmakaya***.

For the equipoise phase, you set yourself as you are without alteration, then enter the state in which the factor of self-knowing rigpa is naked, an empty-luminous-stoppageless self-knowing. Then, when all the doings—all discursive thoughts—that shine forth as the play of its liveliness are, as with the example of an older person watching the games of children, given the freedom to do as they please without the calculations of suppression and furtherance, rejection and adoption, hope and fear, there will come a time when every appearing mind will be just a blip, another evanescent occurrence, another part of the on-off occurrence, part of the general noise[95].

In short, you set your three doors in the uncontrived naturalness of leaving them to be themselves, then come to the uncontrived and cleared-out actuality of mind manifested via naked, cleaned-out[96] rigpa, and this is what is also called "co-emergent wisdom" and "shamatha-vipashyana inseparable", and is the wisdom which is the innate freedom from

---

[95] The image here is the general noise of dharmata. Without the identification of individual dharmas that occurs with rational mind, the experience of dharmata is described in a way that is very similar to a television that has no particular station selected with random hissing noise and strange ghostly shapes randomly appearing on the screen.

[96] Cleared out and cleaned out were described in an earlier note.

elaboration, and the ultimate core of the Secret Mantra Vajra Vehicle's tantra sections, and the factual wisdom[97] of the fourth empowerment, and the very mind of all those who gained accomplishment in India and Tibet and in the Tibetan new and old systems, and the very core of the Hearing Lineage Trilogy. Therefore, the text is saying here, "You ***make a decision*** internally ***that there is*** absolutely ***nothing*** that would be called "rigpa dharmakaya" ***other than that***.

Having thus come to the firm ***decision*** that self-knowing buddha or dharmakaya-wisdom-present-within-oneself-that-has-never-known-confusion buddha is present in your own mindstream, you preserve its state; ***that is the second*** secret line of the ***key point***s.

2.2.3 Explanation of the Way to Build Assurance Over Liberation

The *Three Lines* says,

> *At that point, attachment, anger, happiness, sorrow, and*
> *Every single one of the adventitious discursive thoughts*
> *Are self-recognized and in the state have no ensuing trace.*
> *By identifying their factor of liberation, the dharmakaya,*
> *They, for example like a drawing on water,*

---

[97] Of the four empowerments, the first three show a simile of actual wisdom and the fourth shows the actual fact of wisdom. These are then called the simile and factual wisdoms respectively.

Self-shine-forth self-liberate in an uninterrupted flow.
Whichever one shines forth, it is food for the naked
rigpa-emptiness;
However it moves, it is the liveliness of the
dharmakaya king;
Traceless, it self-purifies. A LA LA!
The way of shining forth being the same as before
compared to
The way of liberation being different is a major key
point.
Without this, meditation is confusion's path;
With this, there is the un-meditated dharmakaya
state.
Assurance built on liberation; that is the third key
point.

This section, quoted above, shows both conduct and fruition. You might have the resting style meditations of abiding mind but without the key point of how to liberate, they cannot elevate you above the upper realms[98]. If your practice does not have the assurance of liberation on shining forth, it will be merely a resting up in the various types of peacefully-abiding mind[99], somewhat like resting up as a long-term guest, as happens with the abiding in absorption

---

[98] All conventional Buddhist meditations involve one-pointed abiding of dualistic samsaric mind. By themselves that cannot take you past the topmost limit of the upper realms of samsara. To go above that, vipashyana, which is the liberating as opposed to resting factor is needed.

[99] Peacefully-abiding mind means all the shamatha type meditations.

for twelve years that is part of the Tirthika's superior conduct[100].

First, you must be introduced, then you must make a decision. After that, you must meditate by engaging in the path of "liberation in the output[101]", and so on. ***At that point***, when something such as a mind of ***attachment*** is produced

---

[100] According to the Buddha, Tirthikas are those who have entered a religion other than Buddhism. They are "tirthika" meaning they have arrived "at the edge" of true spiritual practice (see the *Illuminator Tibetan-English Dictionary* for a full explanation).

The Buddha laid out shila, samadhi, and prajna as the three main trainings for his followers. He called them "higher" to distinguish them from the same or similar trainings of the Tirthikas. Some Tirthikas named their categories "superior" in reply. They have a higher conduct in which emancipation is attained by remaining in one-pointed absorption (dhyana) for twelve years. This is not hypothetical; it is done in India even today. The author is saying here that the abiding-type practices of Buddhism in which there is no vipashyana could be done as a main practice but, over the long term, they would be no more than what the Tirthikas do with their long-term absorption. His point is that abiding meditations in general are nothing more than gymnastic feats of samsaric mind which can give a practitioner a very long and refreshing rest but leave him within samsara.

[101] Liberation in the output is a technical way of speaking that means directly liberating the liveliness of the rigpa—thoughts and all the rest—as it arises. The output of rigpa, which is the luminosity of the rigpa as it manifests, is being mixed with the entity of the rigpa that the practitioner was initially introduced to and has been training in since then.

because of referencing a pleasing object of desire, or strong ***anger*** is produced because of referencing a displeasing object of aversion, or ***happiness*** with the good circumstances—food, clothes, lodging, possessions, and so on—that you have arises, or ***sorrow*** that comes from adverse circumstances—sickness, failure, and so on—arises, it is rigpa standing up right then and there as liveliness. Therefore, you identify all liveliness and play as the wisdom of the ground of liberation[102] and, having done so, the liveliness that has appeared goes on within that space to self-shining-fort- self-liberation.

The way the liberation occurs can be identified both generally and specifically. Speaking generally, there are two ways that it occurs: with and without effort. "With effort" is for those whose appearances come as objects of rational mind. For them, whenever a discursive thought shines forth, there will be identification followed by entrance into the state of rigpa, at which point the mind of purified movement and abiding has been manifested, so, at that point the discursive thought has gone on to liberation. "Without effort" is for those whose appearances come as rigpa appearing of itself to rational mind. For them, the naked rigpa factor is already manifest, so, at that point, every bit of the whole thought-mass that shines forth, self-shines forth and self-dissolves

---

[102] In innermost Great Completion, the ground in general is categorized into two: the ground of liberation and the ground of confusion. The former is the basis for attaining nirvana, the latter the basis for entering samsara. This is fully explained for instance in the first vajra topic of Longchenpa's *Treasury of the Meaning of the Words*.

without ensuing trace within the space of rigpa, like snow falling onto rock.

Specifically, there are five ways of liberation. They are itemized as follows,

> "Being primordial liberation, there is no place to
> be conveyed to;
> Being self-liberation, there is no antidote;
> Being stark liberation, liberation occurs at the
> point of being seen;
> Being shining-forth liberation, there is no
> earlier and later,
> Being single liberation, there is no associate."

In the system of Great Completion, any thought of the five poisons that shines forth goes on to self-liberation and shining-forth liberation. The method used according to mantra is that of making the five poisons into the path, as was done by the forefathers who gained accomplishment previously in India; for example, mahasiddha Lilavajra who as a barmaid made desire into the path, and similarly a low caste person without limbs who made anger into the path, and siddha Lvawapa who made delusion into the path, and the ones who played the games of the childish and made their games into the path.

When you do not have the key point of liberation on shining forth, the mental events of the whole undercurrent of discursive thoughts are accumulating samsaric karma. Thus, this key point of preserving ***every single one of the adventitious discursive thoughts***—every discursive thought subtle or gross, etcetera which might be produced—in shining-forth liberation without trace is important. I will illustrate this using the mindstream of an ordinary person. In that sort of mindstream only three types of thought are possible: good, bad, and indifferent. Of them, the thoughts that are good thoughts are hard to identify[103]. For example, when, because of food, clothes, lodging, personal items, and so on, happy-minded thoughts arise, the idea to put liberation aside arises, there is clinging to the appearance, and karma is accumulated according to the type of clinging involved. Similarly, when such minds as faith and compassion arise, the object which is the Three Jewels and the subject which is the person both are grasped as truly existent. The faith involved also shines forth in the aspect of being truly existent and the compassion is the same. If the rational mind that thinks of death and impermanence arises, the thoughts grasping at the concept tokens[104] of birth and death must be dissolved into the expanse[105]. The same is true for bad thoughts and indifferent thoughts, too. The ground of liberation is the unified knowing of rigpa and its emptiness. What is to be liberated is the three types of thought: good, bad, and indifferent. The mode of liberation is: self liberation; stark liberation; shining-forth liberation; primordial liberation; and single liberation.

If the rigpa factor is not nakedly manifested, you will predominantly be lost through being under the control of the

---

[103] Meaning hard to identify as dharmakaya, to take into the rigpa …

[104] For concept tokens, see the glossary.

[105] The expanse of rigpa, where expanse is a name for the empty side of the rigpa.

undercurrent of discursive thoughts. It is said that equipoise is like a pile of hay and the undercurrent of thought like a stream of water running beneath it, though there is also the point that the thoughts involved have the capacity to accumulate karma[106]. If because of that you deviate into the alaya, that will propel you into the formless realms; if into the alaya consciousness, into the form realms; and if into coarse discursive thought, into the desire realms.

This rigpa in the form of naked empty-luminous-stoppageless rigpa factor has the ability to stop the birthplaces of the three realms. When the rigpa factor does not go into proliferation[107], there is liberation from the desire realm mind; when it does not grasp at the luminosity, there is liberation from the form realm mind; and when it has no thought but its output is unstopped, there is liberation from the formless realm mind. Thus rigpa like this is called, "the mind that universally liberates the three realms".

In that way, no matter which discursive thought shines forth, you do not fall under the control of the undercurrent confusion. Now with this, there is no use of the rational-

---

[106] A small stream of water running under a pile of hay will be perpetually rotting the hay from below but this rot will not be noticed up above. Likewise, the undercurrent of thought—"subconscious gossip" as the vidyadhara Chogyam Trungpa called it—goes unnoticed but is there damaging the equipoise and creating the rot of karmic accumulation at the same time.

[107] Proliferation occurs when dualistic style thoughts are emitted.

mind-made, restrictive type of mindfulness[108] which has the quality of being like a young girl watching out for knots and evenness of thread in wool that she is spinning. Instead, you set yourself so that you are not separate from the mindfulness which belongs to the innate. By doing so, there is "the mindfulness-appearance wisdom sphere" in which discursive thought shines forth and immediately upon doing so the mindfulness that is the thinker of it is liberated into the dharmata; that is the supreme way to preserve the face of mind.

Thus, whichever discursive thought shines forth, it must come out to be rigpa ***self-recognizing*** itself. If every factor which is shining forth and which is to be discarded is set ***in the state*** of the naked rigpa factor, everything that shines forth will proceed to self-shining-forth-self-liberation and, having done to, ***there will be no ensuing trace*** with it. In that way, discursive thought proceeds in the same way as a drawing made on water.

It is important for discursive thought to go on to self-liberation. Mere recognition of the discursive thought as such in which the thought does not become self-liberated, does not cause the continuity of confusion to be cut. Therefore, together with the recognition of the discursive thought, rigpa's own face is starkly put in place whereby discursive thought goes on to self-dissolution or, you can say, ***liberation*** in its own place. At that time, the wisdom present in

---

[108] A restrictive type of mindfulness is one is which you are holding yourself mentally to catch any type of distraction. This dualistic or mental type of mindfulness is tight and restricting by nature.

oneself, ***the dharmakaya***, has been manifested clean and clear, naked and, having been ***identified*** as the wisdom that one is acquainted with from before, has its state preserved. That means that the production of a discursive thought and its liberation have become simultaneous ***like for example a drawing*** made ***on water*** dissolves and collapses of itself immediately it is drawn, so the great rigpa dharmakaya's state now comes as something that is always without meeting and parting[109]. Therefore, no matter which way it shines forth, it is allowed to shine forth without either blocking its onset nor furthering its presence and is thus put into rigpa-empty dharmakaya's state. Through this, the ***self-shining-forth-self-liberating*** continues ***in an uninterrupted flow*** and it becomes impossible for there to be even one thing that will not be liberated within the whole of what does shine forth.

The text says that whichever discursive thought shines forth it is food for the naked rigpa-emptiness. Let us use a human to illustrate the meaning. Any food eaten by a human will serve to increase the strength of his body. Similarly, if what starts out as a strong thought of the five poisons turns into one of the five wisdoms, it will be as has been said about this, "If there are many afflicted thoughts, there are many dharmakaya", meaning that such thoughts will thereby be part of training up or manifesting the dharmakaya rigpa.

---

[109] The great, meaning the primordial, rigpa dharmakaya now comes in the practitioner's experience without meeting and parting. Meeting and parting describes a level of practice at which some good quality has not been finally attained but is still fluctuating in the practitioner's experience of it. Without meeting and parting describes the state in which the practitioner is now fully connected to that good quality all the time.

Thus, whatever shines forth becomes a technique or method through which the intensity of rigpa's brightness is increased. Therefore, Patrul Rinpoche says that ***whichever one*** of those thoughts ***shines forth it is*** like ***food*** that increases the strength ***of the naked, rigpa-emptiness***. With this, he is expressing the idea that, "Naked empty rigpa eats the general mass of thoughts for food".

Thus, what is needed here is to understand that all discursive thought that shines forth is the dharmakaya's liveliness and must be known as rigpa's food. Similarly, ***however*** discursive thought—good, bad, or neutral—***moves*** out[110], ***it*** does not depart from being ***the liveliness*** or play of the rigpa ***dharmakaya king*** which has been fully unveiled into transparency through freeing it from obscuring agents. Thus, all liveliness and play has become great self-shining-forth-self-liberation happening within the rigpa-empty dharmakaya's own space and is liberated without trace.

To do the meditation of acquainting yourself with this, you do that kind of familiarization again and again. Then, at some point, both the grasping at a self of persons that apprehends an I in oneself and the grasping at a self of phenomena that apprehends truth in every phenomenon in the outer and inner—containers and their contents—will be liberated in their own places in rigpa-emptiness's space of the great elaboration-free equality[111]. Thus, the process of

---

110 Discursive thought moves out from the dharmata.

111 Equality is the term meaning the equalness of all phenomena given that they are empty. The space of equality is the space in which all elaborations have vanished.

confusion will be cut. With that, everything that shines forth will be rigpa and only rigpa so it will be as though you could not find anything else even if you searched for it. And, in the same way as all waves are none other than the ocean, everything that shines forth will go, within the space of rigpa's wisdom, on to being ***traceless, self-purified***, self-dissolved. At that point, like not being able to find ordinary earth and rocks on an island made of gold, everything that shines forth, merging into non-duality within the space of the single unique sphere of rigpa-emptiness, will be the great dharmakaya that spreads throughout all. Therefore, the text says, "***A LA LA***" meaning how utterly wonderful!

Similarly, in the post-attainment phase, discursive thinking, with its ***way of shining forth being the same as before***, continues on with various thoughts being elaborated but, as has been said in reference to this point,

> "The shining forth involved is like that of
> ordinary thought;
> The liberation involved is the yoga's special
> feature."

In other words, "discursive thought shines forth as meditation" and because of that, everything that shines forth is meditation. It is like this: no matter which way it shines forth, it does not get stopped at the level of dwelling and no matter how it dwells, the shining-forth factor is stoppageless[112].

---

[112] Rigpa never just sits as its space-like entity but is constantly expressive; it is nothing and everything without any contradiction between the two. The way it happens is that it shines forth

(continued...)

It does not need to be something in which there is no shining forth occurring but needs to be something in which there is not even one bit of the shining forth not liberated. Ordinarily, clinging appears in accordance with the sort of discursive thought that shines forth and then karma is accumulated in accordance with the clinging. However, in the context of this yoga, no matter which way discursive though shines forth, there is nothing to be lost for the rigpa and nothing to be gained for the discursive thought, so the situation is like that of a thief who has entered an empty house. In that case, discursive thought has not the slightest power to do anything, for example, when the warmth of spring has arrived in the fields, even if there is a hail storm, the menace of its coldness is neutralized and it has no power. And, as in the example of a hessian rope that has been burned in fire, no accumulation of karma could occur[113].

With this, confused appearance goes into self-collapse. In this process, rigpa is able to defeat the confused appearances seen over there, yet they are not at all able to defeat the rigpa known over here—the rigpa is like a diamond sword and a vajra.

---

[112](...continued)
and comes into being but does not get stuck there; instead, it dissolves of itself.

[113] A hessian rope can do things; it can act, which is the meaning of the word karma, "action". A hessian rope will be totally consumed by fire after which it will be completely incapable of action. At this level of practice, when a discursive thought is self-liberated, there is no possibility of it having the power to act, that is, to create karma.

Continuing on with the text: first discursive thought is liberated by recognition, which is like meeting a man you are acquainted with from before; in the middle, discursive thought self liberates of itself, like a snake uncoils; finally, discursive thought is liberated in being neither helpful nor harmful, like a thief who has entered an empty house. Understand that ***this mode of liberation being different*** from the way of shining forth has the feature of these three ways of liberation; this ***is a major key point***. In meditation, the way that a discursive thought shines forth is the same as before, but, ***without this*** feature of the way of liberation in which anything that shines forth goes on to self-shining-forth-self-liberation, ***meditation is confusion's path***. This has been referred to like this,

> "Knowing how to meditate but not how to
> liberate—
> How is that different from the absorption
> gods[114]?"

and Zhabkar said,

> "Just to abide is the same as the absorption gods,
> Just to move is the same as ordinary awareness;
> You can meditate on those but you won't attain
> buddhahood by doing so."

Just abiding, just recognizing abiding and movement, and just sealing with emptiness are three points of deviation. If you develop an assurance of meditation which is just an absorption in which mind is abiding, the result will be that, immediately upon death, you will be born into the

---

[114] The absorption gods are those living in the dhyana absorptions, that is, the gods of the form and formless realms.

absorption abodes of the upper realms. If you have nothing except just recognition of abiding and movement, because that is the ordinary awareness of confused thought, there will be no difference between your mind and an ordinary being's mind. Sealing done as an act of rational mind that thinks, "Everything is empty", will mean that you have become lost in sealing with emptiness, with the result that, when you meet bad circumstances, you will rouse thoughts of the poisons. This has been described like this:

> "When your belly is full and you are warmed by
> the sun, you have the appearance of dharma;
> When bad circumstances befall you, you are an
> ordinary person!"

and,

> "If the view has been stolen by an old thief,
> Your conduct has been locked up; the old thief
> has you in his service!"

There are four ways of liberation. The ground is situated as something primordially without shift, which is primordial liberation. There is the way appearances happen to a person but there is also subsidence of grasping at the four extremes into the expanse, which is liberation of extremes. When rigpa is woken in the centre of the heart, the entire mass of thoughts that shine forth are liberated without any mind being involved or roused, which is self-liberation. Not abandoning appearances there is liberation right on the appearance and not abandoning movement there is liberation right on the movement, which is stark liberation.

To go further with this, it is taught that self-liberation can be designated as equipoise and, when the seal of concentration is broken, stark liberation can be designated as post-attainment. We could continue to apply other names such as single liberation, and so on. However, to sum this up: if you ***have this*** mode of liberation in which discursive thought self-liberates and purifies itself so that it is gone without trace, ***then*** every affliction and every discursive thought will stand up as dharmakaya. Thus confused thought is being purified into wisdom, bad circumstances are coming forth as assistants, afflictions are being made into the path, samsara without being abandoned is being liberated in its own place, and ***there is*** liberation from the fetters of becoming[115] and peace. The stronghold, without meeting and parting, has been seized in ***the*** great primordial liberation alpha-purity, ***un-meditated dharmakaya state***.

Thus, here, afflictions are not abandoned as they are with shravakas, are not used for training as they are with bodhicitta, and are not transformed as they are with mantra. Instead, the state in which what shines-forth self-liberates is preserved, and that is the feature of Nature Great Completion.

If you do not have the assurance of that sort of liberation, then, no matter how high your view, no matter how good your meditation, it will not benefit your mind and will not become an antidote for the afflictions, therefore, being without it is not a true path. If you have this key point of self-shining-forth-self-liberation, you might not have the

---

[115] For becoming, see the glossary.

approach of apprehending a high view or having the foci of profound meditations, but it is impossible that your mindstream will not be liberated from the fetters of dualistic grasping. Like not being able to find ordinary earth and rocks on an island made of gold even if you search for such, abiding and movement, and discursive thought that arises shines forth as meditation and therefore cannot be found as confusion *per se* even if you search for it. Whether something functions as a key point of meditation or not depends on that alone; it is like a reference line that demarcates the two sides of the situation.

Similarly, it is one's conduct that is used to assess the extent of training. The extent of training is known through whether or not there is renunciation towards samsara, trust in cause and effect, compassion for sentient beings, pure perception towards situations, devotion towards the guru, great love for close dharma associates, prajna come from meditation, and so on.

Starting with that kind of view and then having extended the continuity of the meditation so that it goes on without break day and night, that is to say, having ***built***, on top of the introduction given earlier by the guru, ***assurance*** that is based ***on liberation; that is the third*** line, concerning the secret, of the ***key points***.

❀ ❀ ❀

Next there is a summary of the meaning of threefold view, meditation, and conduct. In general, for Great Completion there is view, meditation, and conduct. Here, in addition, there is also the basis of the accomplishment of the three kayas, the fruition, to make four, and then the samaya that prevents you from parting from all that to make a set of five. You must keep yourself in these five on the basis of the one, fully unveiled transparent rigpa.

Similarly, ground, path, and fruition are three but for these too there is nothing but the one rigpa. The ground comes from the aspect of the primordial situation of the innate wisdom that abides in your mindstream. The path comes from the aspect of the present in which you practice what the guru has introduced you to. The fruition comes from the aspect of the two obscurations having dissolved into the space of the ground.

Now that does not follow the way of the mainstream texts[116] in which the view in regard to all dharmas is determined through evaluation with authentic statement, reasoning, and logic. Here instead, the innate—because it has been primordially present in the mindstream—factual wisdom, is awakened right in the present using the guru's foremost instructions and the fact, in direct perception, of the naked rigpa factor is introduced. In this approach, the matter is decided internally[117]; if a liberation from the shackles of "It's this, it's not that" occurs, then that is the view. Thus, the

---

[116] The main texts of Buddhism in general, for example the many sutra texts such as *Entrance to the Middle Way* by Chandrakirti, and so on.

[117] To determine the view using scripture, logic, and so on is to determine it externally.

practice of this Atiyoga, Thorough Cut view does not depend on age and being old or young, on one's amount of prajna being great or small, on sharpness or dullness of faculty, on one's karma being good or bad, and so on; rather, anyone who realizes self-arising rigpa in reliance on faith, devotion, and perseverance, will be liberated.

3. Conclusion

There are three parts to this: summary of the meaning; advice that this is extremely profound advice; and a most significant point, that it has a command seal.

3.1 Summary of the Meaning

The *Three Lines* says,

> *For the view having the three key points there are*
> *The meditation of connecting wisdom and love and*
> *The assistive general conduct of the conquerors' sons.*

This view having like that ***the three key points*** of introduction to oneself, decision on one thing, and assurance built on liberation is the view of the fruition vehicle at the very peak of the nine vehicles. Just as Mt. Meru, the king of mountains, sits at the very peak of all mountains of the world and is the king of mountains, so this vehicle also is the king of all vehicles. Thus, if it were the case that all the vehicles below it did not sooner or later connect ***to this view***, then the fruition of the rank of a buddha would not be possible. Moreover, just as it is impossible for the seven signs of sovereignty and the armed forces that belong to a wheel-wielding king not to go where he goes, so all lesser vehicles support or act as assistants to this fruition vehicle's path and always travel with it. The *Condensed*[118] says,

> "There is the road which a wheel-wielding king always takes
> And due to being such a road, the seven precious things and all armed forces will go on it;
> Where this Prajnaparamita of the conqueror goes, this goes,
> And due to being so, all the good qualities of dharma will go with it."

In other words, all vehicles are branches of this one and go with it as assistants who aid its realization.

Generally speaking, both alpha-purity-Thorough-Cut's rigpa and spontaneous-presence-Direct-Crossing's prajna-self-arising lamp have the same meaning: alpha-purity rigpa is the prajna self-arising lamp's entity; its output is the vajra chains; and its liveliness is prajna risen from meditation[119]. Thus, if you have met rigpa in the introduction and acquainted yourself with it through familiarization, the liveliness which is prajna risen from meditation will have

---

[118] Skt. ārya prajñāpāramitā samchayagātha sūtra. One of the many Prajnaparamita sutras. This one sums up the whole Prajnaparamita in sixty, four line verses.

[119] This is a topic of Direct Crossing in which the relationship between the prajna self-arising lamp and rigpa is clarified. It is explained, for example, in Jigmey Lingpa's *Guidebook to the Stages of the Path called Highest Wisdom*, a translation of which is available through Padma Karpo Translation Committee.

blazed[120]. Then the mode of individual phenomena's appearance together with the space of ***knowledge*** of dharmata's actuality just as it is, will be bursting forth like a summertime lake[121] ***and*** emptiness having a core of compassion will be shining forth such that the ***love*** belonging to compassion for sentient beings who have not realized this will be happening without need of concept-driven effort. Thus, the state to be preserved—the state of meditation in which that sort of expanse of emptiness that possesses the excellence of all superficies[122] of the great original emptiness and the love of great compassion are being unified, that is, are being ***connected*** together—is the ***meditation***. ***And***, at the point when the key point of path—which is the unifying together of

---

[120] The way in which this current sentence follows on from the previous one will be hard to see unless one has extensive teachings on Direct Crossing. Simply stated, the liveliness of the rigpa is the point that connects rigpa meditation to the meditation of Direct Crossing. If you have met rigpa, practised it, and reached the point where it has really blazed, then you will have reached the finality of the path of both Thorough Cut and Direct Crossing. The rest of the paragraph describes, from a Thorough Cut perspective, what that final realization will be like.

[121] In Tibet, in the summer, the lakes are overflowing as water gushes into them from the melting snows and glaciers.

[122] Tib. rnam pa: in discussions of mind, a distinction is made between the entity of mind, which is a mere knower, and the superficial things that appear on its surface, which are known by it. Superficies are all the specifics that constitute appearance, for example, the colour white within a moment of visual consciousness, the sound heard within an ear consciousness, and so on.

emptiness and compassion like that—has been manifested, then, in equipoise, there will be the non-referential wisdom accumulation which is exemplified as the sun, and in post-attainment there will be the referential merit accumulation of the ***general conduct of the conquerors' sons***—the ocean-like conduct of the six paramitas, and so on—which shines forth from the play of rigpa's liveliness and which is exemplified as the light rays that are the elaborations of the sun. That general conduct of the conqueror's sons will be shining forth as an ***assistant*** that works to bring the peace which is the cessation of the extremes.

3.2 Advice That this is Extremely Profound Instruction

The *Three Lines* says,

> *Even a conference of the conquerors of the three times*
> *Would not find an oral instruction superior to this.*
> *Rigpa's liveliness, the dharmakaya treasure revealer,*
> *Takes the treasure from the space of prajna;*
> *This is not like the quintessences of earth and rock.*
> *It is the testament of Garab Dorje;*
> *It is the three lineage's enlightened mind-juice.*

Even if all ***the conquerors of the three times*** were to join together in ***a conference*** and discuss the matter, they ***would not come out with an*** oral instruction more profound than this oral instruction whose three lines strike the key points. It is the understanding of all the buddhas of the three times; the heart blood of one hundred thousand feminine dakinis; the very core of the eighty-four thousand-fold dharma heap[123]; the king at the summit of all vehicles; like the heart

---

[123] The dharma heap, consisting of eighty-four thousand indi-
(continued...)

extracted from all the tantra sections; the quintessence of all foremost instructions; the key points of all collections of excellent speech rolled into one; and, like butter, the essence obtained from churning milk. Thus, there is no other ***oral instruction superior to this***, the meaning of Luminosity Great Completion's Longchen Nyingthig contained in a compilation of key points that is like a concoction of medicines, expressed in so few words and expressing such profound meaning.

Abu Rinpoche's[124] teaching here came forth from his ***rigpa's liveliness*** as a mind treasure so he calls that liveliness "***the dharmakaya treasure revealer***". ***Takes the treasure*** refers to his way of just suddenly speaking whatever came forth ***from*** his own ***space of*** the ***prajna*** that realizes lack of self, a space which is space-like and all-pervasive[125]. There are worldly treasures, he says, which are extracted ***quintessences of earth and rock*** that can have immediate effects such as elimination of failures and poverty in this life but, he says, ***this is not like*** them. This style of his was recorded by Nyag Lama Sogyal who said,

> "I offered Abu Rinpoche a treasure casket and he, not showing any joy over it, said this.

---

[123](...continued)
vidual teachings, is the entirety of the Buddha's teaching.

[124] Dza Patrul often referred to himself as Abu in his writings and people referred to him after that as Abu Rinpoche.

[125] "His space" is his own space of internal experience. Prajna which realizes lack of self is experienced as a space-like emptiness which is all-pervasive.

> ‘It is alright to get it this sort of thing and alright not to get it, too. Why is that? The confused thoughts belonging to the mind of the three poisons brought forth by ignorance that grasps at truth are tougher even than Red Rock Fortress[126]. The three temporary experiences of bliss, clarity, and no-thought are deeper than the Blue Lake[127]. It is difficult to break this seal. It is difficult to fathom this depth. Therefore, the guru’s foremost instructions and your own tool of prajna should be used to smash this rock mountain of confused thoughts of the mind of the three poisons brought forth by ignorance grasping at truth. They should be used to punch right through to the depth, deep as the Blue Lake, of these three temporary experiences. If you manage that, then you will have taken naked self-arising wisdom, the ultimate mind of Samantabhadra, which is the superfactual treasure out from the box of alaya and eightfold consciousness. To take out that sort of treasure is wondrous indeed!’”

When vidyadhara Garab Dorje went to body nirvana, at the neck of Tan Tig river, Master Manjushrimitra supplicated him with words of longing. From the midst of rainbow light of the five colours, Master ***Garab Dorje’s*** illusory wisdom body extended its right arm as far as the elbow and in a casket made of five precious things on a sheet of lapis

---

[126] The name of a mountain in Tibet composed only of rocky crags made of reddish granite.

[127] A very large and deep lake in the North-east of Tibet.

lazuli and in letters spontaneously written in refined gold, this, which is his ***testament*** of the Three Lines that Strike the Key Points, came forth. Master Manjushrimitra saw it and, with just that, the minds of master and disciple merged inseparable, and the meaning just exactly as it is of this profound oral instruction was realized in the disciple's mindstream.

All-Knowing Dharma King Longchen Rabjam, manifested the mind of Dharmas Exhausted that goes with that[128]. Having done so, he became a manifest complete buddha in his life. When he went to body nirvana, he left behind bones and relics as an offering to migrators. Up to this point the transmission occurred through the conquerors' mind lineage.

A little more than five hundred years after All-Knowing One's nirvana, vidyadhara Jigmey Lingpa practised in the forests of Samye Chimphu for three years. During that time, he one-pointedly supplicated the Great All-knowing One and, using the method for accomplishing the guru called *Thigle Gyachen*[129], saw the face of the Great All-knowing One's illusory body three times. That transmission occurred through the vidyadhara sign lineage.

Jigmey Lingpa in turn instructed Jigmey Gyalwa'i Nyugu who met the dharmata in direct perception; that transmission occurred through the person's aural lineage. That is

---

[128] Garab Dorje's Three Lines that Strike the Key Points.

[129] The innermost of guru yoga of Longchenpa.

the way in which ***it is the three lineage's enlightened mind-juice***.

3.3 A Most Significant Point, that it has a Command Seal

The *Three Lines* says,

> *It is entrusted to heart sons. Sealed!*
> *It is the profound meaning. It is the story of the heart's*
> *Heart story. It is the key points of the meaning.*
> *Do not let the key points of the meaning disappear.*
> *Do not let the oral instructions leak away.*
> *This is the feature of the expert, glorious king!*

These profound foremost instructions, which are like the quintessence (Nyingthig), are not suitable to be shown to anyone who is not a suitable vessel, that is, to someone who will not practise it. On the other hand, if it were not shown to persons who are suitable vessels for it, that is, to beings who will cherish this oral instruction as though it were their eyes, that would be a great loss, so the text says that ***it is entrusted*** out of love ***to*** fortunate disciples, those who are like ***heart sons***. "Entrusted" means that a ***seal*** of secrecy has been placed on it so that it will not be shown to those who are not suitable vessels for it and also that it you should practise it*!*

When he says, "This, which has the ***profound meanings*** of the secret compiled together, shows those meanings by condensing them down into a few, clearly-expressed words", he is saying that he has openly stated ***the story of the heart***[130]

[130] Here, "story of the heart" means talk of the essence; he has told the very core meaning to his disciples.

for those persons who are his fortunate disciples that are suitable vessels. This oral instruction is a treasure he is giving, esteemed and cherished like the eyes in the head and the heart in the chest, therefore it is talk given from the heart, a ***heart story***[131].

The key points of the meaning of the Hearing Lineage Trilogy that came from the Great All-knowing One are included in this too, therefore ***it is the key points of the meaning***. Cherish these profound ***key points of the meaning*** which are like a jewel which provides all wants and needs, which fulfills all wishes, and with that, ***do not*** throw them away by not practising them and let ***them disappear*** in meaningless waste! You have heard this profound ***oral instruction***, which is like a medicinal nectar that can revive the dead, with your own ears; not to practise it one-pointedly would be to allow the container to break and the medicine leak away; ***do not let it leak away*** like that*!*

That is the end of showing ***the feature of the*** one who, being an ***expert*** who has gone to the other shore of the ocean-like body of literature of the areas of knowledge within sutra and tantra, is the Shri or ***Glorious King***[132].

---

[131] Here, "heart story" means "the talk of love"; he has spoken with love to his disciples.

[132] Glorious King is a name that Dza Patrul used to refer to himself as someone who was a glorious king of knowledge. Here it explains his name and this also helps to explain the title of his text *The Feature of the Expert, Glorious King*.

I have recorded above in writing what my holy guru said together with my own thoughts about it. However, given that I have not the slightest good quality, I do sit here scared by the thought that it could be a cause of concern for the holy ones. Nonetheless, pressed by my nephew Dampa Tsultrim Zangpo and the others with whom I have a previous karmic connection—dearest Karlo, nephew Namdren, and khenpos Thubcho, Chodrag, and Lodro—and not being able to refuse them, this wandering beggar-type with the name Tenpa wrote this down.

Virtue. Virtue. Virtue. Sarva mangalam.

GLOSSARY

Actuality, Tib. gnas lugs: A key term in both sūtra and tantra and one of a pair of terms, the other being apparent reality (Tib. snang lugs). The two terms are used when determining the reality of a situation. The actuality of any given situation is how (lugs) the situation actuality sits or is present (gnas); the apparent reality is how any given situation appears to an observer. Something could appear in many different ways, depending on the circumstances at the time and on the being perceiving it but, regardless of those circumstances, it will always have its own actuality of how it really is. The term actuality is frequently used in Mahāmudrā and Great Completion teachings to mean the fundamental reality of any given phenomenon or situation before any deluded mind alters it and makes it appear differently.

Adventitious, Tib. glo bur: This term has the connotations of popping up on the surface of something and of not being part of that thing. Therefore, even though it is often translated as "sudden", that only conveys half of the meaning. In Buddhist literature, something adventitious comes up as a surface event and disappears again precisely because it is not actually part of the thing on whose surface it appeared. It is frequently used in relation to the afflictions because they pop up on the surface of the mind of buddha-nature but are not part of the buddha-nature itself.

Affliction, Skt. kleśha, Tib. nyon mongs: This term is usually translated as emotion or disturbing emotion, etcetera, but the Buddha was very specific about the meaning of this word. When the Buddha referred to the emotions, meaning a movement of mind, he did not refer to them as such but called them "kleśha" in Sanskrit, meaning exactly "affliction". It is a basic part of the Buddhist teaching that emotions afflict beings, giving them problems at the time and causing more problems in the future.

Alaya, Skt. ālaya, Tib. kun gzhi: This term, if translated, is usually translated as all-base or thereabouts. It is a Sanskrit term that means a range that underlies and forms a basis for something else. In Buddhist teaching, it means a particular level of mind that sits beneath all other levels of mind. However, it is used in several different ways in the Buddhist teaching and changes to a different meaning in each case. In the Great Completion teachings, an important distinction is made between ālaya alone and ālaya consciousness.

Alpha purity, Tib. ka dag: A Great Completion term meaning purity that is there from the first, that is, primordial purity. There are many terms in Buddhism that express the notion of "primordial purity" but this one is unique to the Great Completion teaching. The term "alpha purity" matches the Tibetan term both literally and in meaning.

Alteration, altered: Same as contrivance *q.v.*

Assurance, Tib. gdeng: Although often translated as confidence, this term means assurance with all of the extra meaning conveyed by that term. A bird might be confident of its ability to fly but more than that, it has the assurance that it will not fall to the ground because of knowing that it has wings and the training to use them. Similarly, a person might be confident that they could liberate the afflictions but not assured of doing so because of lack of training or other causes. However, a person who has accumulated the causes to be able to liberate afflictions trained is assured of the ability to do so.

Becoming, Skt. bhāvanā, Tib. srid pa: Becoming refers to the style of existence that sentient beings have within saṃsāra. Beings in saṃsāra have a samsaric existence but, more than that, they are constantly in a state of becoming. They are constantly becoming this type of being or that type of being in this abode or that, as they are driven along without choice by the karmic process that drives samsaric existence.

Bliss, clarity, and no-thought, Tib. bde gsal mi rtog pa: A practitioner who engages in practice will have signs of that practice appear as various types of temporary experience. Most commonly, three types of experience are met with: bliss, clarity, and no-thought. Bliss is an ease of body or mind or both, clarity is heightened knowing of mind, and no-thought is an absence of thought that happens in the mind. The three are usually mentioned when discussing the passing experiences that arise because of practising meditation but there is also a way of describing them as final experiences of realization.

Bodhicitta: See under enlightenment mind.

Clinging, Tib. zhen pa: In Buddhism, this term refers specifically to the twofold process of dualistic mind mis-taking things that are not true, not pure, as true, pure, etcetera and then, because of seeing them as highly desirable even though they are not, attaching itself to or clinging to those things. This type of clinging acts as a kind of glue that keeps a person joined to the unsatisfactory things of cyclic existence because of mistakenly seeing them as desirable.

Compassionate activity, Tib. thugs rje: This does not mean compassionate activity in general. Rather, it is a specific term of the most profound level of teachings of Mahāmudrā and

Great Completion. These teachings describe innate wisdom as having three characteristics. The third characteristic is this compassionate activity. It refers to the fact that wisdom spontaneously does whatever needs to be done, throughout all reaches of time and space, for all beings. Although it includes the word "compassion" in its name, it is more primordial than that. It is the dynamic quality of enlightenment which choicelessly, ceaselessly, spontaneously, and pervasively acts to benefit others. The term is often used in discussions of Great Completion and essence Mahāmudrā.

Concept tokens, Tib. mtshan ma: This is the technical name for the structures or concepts which function as the words of conceptual mind's language. For example, a table seen in direct visual perception will have no conceptual tokens involved with knowing it. However, when thought becomes involved and there is the thought "table" in an inferential or conceptual perception of the table, the name-tag "table" will be used to reference the table and that name tag is the conceptual token.

Although we usually reference phenomena via these concepts, the phenomena are not the dualistically referenced things we think of them as being. The actual fact of the phenomena is quite different from the conceptual tokens used to discursively think about them and is known by wisdom rather than concept-based mind. Therefore, this term is often used in Buddhist literature to signify that samsaric mind is involved rather than non-dualistic wisdom.

Confusion, Tib. 'khrul pa: In Buddhism, this term mostly refers to the fundamental confusion of taking things the wrong way that happens because of fundamental ignorance, although it can also have the more general meaning of having lots of thoughts and being confused about it. In the first case, it is defined like this "Confusion is the appearance to rational mind of something being present when it is not" and refers, for example, to seeing an object, such as a table, as being truly present when in fact it is present only as mere, interdependent appearance.

Contrivance, contrived, Tib. bcos pa: A term meaning that something has been altered from its native state.

Cyclic existence: See under saṃsāra.

Dharmadhatu, Skt. dharmadhātu, Tib. chos kyi dbyings: This is the name for the range or basic space in which all dharmas, meaning all phenomena, come into being. If a flower bed is the place where flowers grow and are found, the dharmadhātu is the dharma or phenomena bed in which all phenomena come into being and are found. The term is used in all levels of Buddhist teaching with that basis meaning but the explanation of it becomes more profound as the teaching becomes more profound. In Great Completion and Mahāmudrā, it is the all-pervading sphere of luminosity-wisdom, given that luminosity is where phenomena arise and that the luminosity is none other than wisdom.

Dharmakaya, Skt. dharmakāya, Tib. chos sku: In the general teachings of Buddhism, this refers to the mind of a buddha, with "dharma" meaning reality and "kāya" meaning body. In the Thorough Cut practice of Great Completion it additionally has the special meaning of being the means by which one rapidly imposes liberation on oneself.

Dharmata, Tib. chos nyid: This is a general term meaning the way that something is, and can be applied to anything at all; it is similar in meaning to "actuality" *q.v.* For example, the dharmatā of water is wetness and the dharmatā of the becoming bardo is a place where beings are in a saṃsāric, or becoming mode, prior to entering a nature bardo. It is used frequently in Tibetan Buddhism to mean "the dharmatā of reality" but that is a specific case of the much larger meaning of the term. To read texts which use this term successfully, one has to understand that the term has a general meaning and then see how that applies in context.

Dhyana, Skt. dhyāna, Tib. bsam gtan: A Sanskrit term technically meaning all types of mental absorption. Mental absorptions cultivated in the human realm generally result in births in the form realms which are deep forms of concentration in themselves. The practices of mental absorption done in the human realm and the godly existences of the form realm that result from them both are named "dhyāna". The Buddha repeatedly pointed out that the dhyānas were a side-track to emancipation from cyclic existence.

In a more general way, the term also means meditation in general where one is concentrating on something as a way of developing oneself spiritually. Texts on Great Completion often use the word in this sense when making the point that attempts to meditate on anything are the very opposite of the Great Completion practice and will inevitably keep the practitioner within saṃsāra.

Direct Crossing, Tib. thod rgal: The name of the two main practices of the innermost level of Great Completion. The other one is Thorough Cut *q.v.*

Discursive thought, Skt. vikalpa, Tib. rnam rtog: This means more than just the superficial thought that is heard as a voice in the head. It includes the entirety of conceptual process that arises due to mind contacting any object of any of the senses. The Sanskrit and Tibetan literally mean "(dualistic) thought (that arises from the mind wandering among the) various (superficies perceived in the doors of the senses)".

Effort, Conceptual effort, Tib. rtsol ba: In Buddhism, this term usually does not merely mean effort but has the specific connotation of effort of dualistic mind. In that case, it is effort that is produced by and functions specifically within the context of dualistic concept. For example, the term "mindfulness with effort" specifically means "a type of mindfulness that is occurring within the context of dualistic mind and its various operations". The term "effortless" is often used in Mahāmudrā and Great Completion to mean a way of being in which dualistic mind has been abandoned and, therefore, has with it none of the effort of dualistic mind.

Elaboration, Tib. spro ba: A general name for what is given off by dualistic mind as it goes about its conceptual process. In general, elaborations prevent a person from seeing emptiness directly. Freedom from elaborations implies direct sight of emptiness.

Enlightenment mind, Skt. bodhicitta, Tib. byang chub sems: A key term of the Great Vehicle. It is the type of mind that is connected not with the lesser enlightenment of an arhat but the enlightenment of a truly complete buddha. As such, it is a mind which is connected with the aim of bringing all sentient beings to that same level of buddhahood. A person who has this mind has entered the Great Vehicle and is either a bodhisatva or a buddha.

It is important to understand that the term is used to refer equally to the minds of all levels of bodhisatva on the path to buddhahood and to the mind of a buddha who has completed the path. Therefore it is not "mind striving for enlightenment" as is so often translated but "enlightenment mind", meaning that kind of mind which is connected with the full enlightenment of a truly complete buddha and which is present in all those who belong to the Great Vehicle. The term is used in the conventional Great Vehicle and also in the Vajra Vehicle. In the Vajra Vehicle, there are some special uses of the term where substances of the pure aspect of the subtle physical body are understood to be manifestations of enlightenment mind.

Entity, Tib. ngo bo: The entity of something is just exactly what that thing is. In English we would often simply say "thing" rather than entity. However, in Buddhism, "thing" has a very specific meaning rather than the general meaning that it has in English. It has become common to translate this term as "essence". However, in most cases "entity", meaning what a thing is rather than an essence of that thing, is the correct translation for this term.

Equipoise and post-attainment, Tib. mnyam bzhag and rjes thob: Although often called "meditation and post-meditation", the actual term is "equipoise and post-attainment". There is great meaning in the actual wording which is lost by the looser translation.

Essence, Tib. ngo bo: This is a key term used throughout Buddhist theory. The original in Sanskrit and the term in Tibetan, too, has both meanings of "essence" and "entity". In some situations the term has more the first meaning and in others, the second. For example, when speaking of mind and mind's essence, it is referring to the core or essential part within mind. On the other hand, when speaking of something such as fire, one can speak of the entity, fire, and its characteristics, such as heat, and so on; in this case, the term does not mean essence but means that thing, what it actually is. See also under entity.

Expanse, Skt. dhātu, Tib. dbyings: A Sanskrit term with over twenty meanings. Many of those meanings are also present in the Tibetan equivalent. In the Vajra Vehicle teachings it is used as a replacement for the term emptiness that conveys a non-theoretical sense of the experience of emptiness. When used this way, it has the sense "expanse" because emptiness is experienced as an expanse in which all phenomena appear.

Fictional, Skt. saṃvṛti, Tib. kun rdzob: This term is paired with the term "superfactual" *q.v.* Until now these two terms have been translated as "relative" and "absolute" but these translations are nothing like the original terms. These terms are extremely important in the Buddhist teaching so it is very important that they be corrected, but more than that, if the actual meaning of these terms is not presented, then the teaching connected with them cannot be understood.

The Sanskrit term saṃvṛti means a deliberate invention, a fiction, a hoax. It refers to the mind of ignorance which, because of being obscured and so not seeing suchness, is not true but a fiction. The things that appear to that ignorance are therefore fictional. Nonetheless, the beings who live in this ignorance believe that the things that appear to them through the filter of ignorance are true, are real. Therefore, these beings live in fictional truth.

Focus, foci, Tib. gtad so: A particular issue that rational mind is focussing on. Sometimes this term is used to infer the presence of dualistic mind.

Foremost instruction, Skt. upadeśha, Tib. man ngag: There are several types of instruction mentioned in Buddhist literature: there is the general level of instruction which is the meaning contained in the words of the texts of the tradition; on a more personal and direct level there is oral instruction which has been passed down from teacher to student from the time of the buddha; and on the most profound level there is upadeśha which are not only oral instructions provided by one's guru but are special, core instructions that come out of personal experience and which convey the teaching concisely and with the full weight of personal experience. Upadeśha are crucial to the Vajra Vehicle because these are the special way of passing on the profound instructions needed for the student's realization.

Fortunate, fortunate person, Tib. skal ldan: A person who has accumulated the karma needed to be involved with any given practice of dharma. This term is especially used in relation to the Vajra Vehicle whose practices are generally very hard to meet with. To meet with them, a person has to have developed all of the karma needed for such a rare opportunity, and this kind of person is then called "a fortunate one" or "fortunate person".

Ground, Tib. gzhi: This is the first member of the formulation of ground, path, and fruition. Ground, path, and fruition is the way that the teachings of the path of oral instruction belonging to the Vajra Vehicle are presented to students. Ground refers to the basic situation as it is.

Introduction and To Introduce, Tib. ngos sprad and ngos sprod pa respectively: This pair of terms is usually translated today as "pointing out" "and "to point out" but this is a mistake that has, unfortunately, become entrenched. The terms are the standard terms used in day to day life for the situation in which one person introduces another person to someone or something. They are the exact same words as our English "introduction" and "to introduce".

In the Vajra Vehicle, these terms are specifically used for the situation in which one person introduces another person to the nature of his own mind. Now there is a term in Tibetan for "pointing out" but that term is never used for this purpose because in this case noone points out anything. Rather, a person is introduced by another person to a part of himself that he has forgotten about.

Key points, Tib. gnad: Key points are those places in one's being that one works, like pressing buttons, in order to get some desired effect. For example, in meditation, there are key points of the body; by adjusting those key points, the mind is brought closer to reality and the meditation is thus assisted.

In general, this term is used in Buddhist meditation instruction but it is, in particular, part of the special vocabulary of the Great Completion teachings. Overall, the Great Completion teachings are given as a series of key points that must be attended to in order to bring forth the various realizations of the path.

Liveliness, Tib. rtsal: A key term in both Mahāmudrā and Great Completion. The term means the ability that something has to express itself. In the case of rigpa, it refers to how the rigpa actually comes out into expression. The term is sometimes translated as "display" but that is not right. It is not merely the display that is being talked about here but the fact that something has the ability to express itself in a certain way. Another English word that fits the meaning, though one which is drier than "liveliness", is "expressivity". In the end, given the way that this term is actually used in the higher tantras, it refers to the liveliness of whatever is being referred to, usually rigpa.

Luminosity, Skt. prabhāsvara, Tib. 'od gsal ba: The core of mind has two aspects: an emptiness factor and a knowing factor. Luminosity is a metaphor for the fundamental knowing quality of the essence of mind. It is sometimes translated as "clear light" but that is a mistake that comes from not understanding the etymology of the word. It does not refer to a light that has the quality of clearness (something that makes no sense, actually!) but refers to the illuminative property which is the hallmark of mind. Mind knows, that is what it does. Metaphorically, it is a luminosity that illuminates its own content. In both Sanskrit and Tibetan Buddhist literature, the term is frequently abbreviated just to gsal ba, "clarity", with the same meaning.

Mind, Skt. chitta, Tib. sems: The complicated process of mind which occurs because there is ignorance. This sort of mind is a samsaric phenomenon. It is a dualistic mind.

Mindfulness, Tib. dran pa: A particular mental event, one that has the ability to keep mind on its object. Together with alertness, it is one of the two causes of developing śhamatha. See under alertness.

Mindness, Skt. chittatā, Tib. sems nyid: Mindness is a specific term of the tantras. It is one of many terms meaning the essence of mind or the nature of mind. It conveys the sense of "what mind is at its very core". It has sometimes been translated as "mind itself" but that is a misunderstanding of the Tibetan word "nyid". The term does not mean "that thing mind" where mind refers to dualistic mind. Rather, it means the very core of dualistic mind, what mind is at root, without all of the dualistic baggage.

Mindness is a path term. It refers to exactly the same thing as "actuality" or "actuality of mind" which is a ground term but does so from the practitioner's perspective. It conveys the sense to a practitioner that he might still have baggage of dualistic mind that has not yet been purified but that there is a core to that mind that he can work with.

Nature Great Completion, Tib. rang bzhin rdzogs pa chen po: This is one of several names for Great Completion that emphasizes the path aspect of Great Completion. It is not "natural great completion" nor is it "the true nature Great Completion" as commonly seen. In terms of grammar, the first term is the noun "nature" not the adjective "natural". In terms of meaning, the noun nature is used because it refers to the nature aspect in particular of the three characteristics of the essence of mind—entity, nature, and unstopped compassionate activity—used to describe Great Completion as experienced by the practitioner. Thus, this name refers to the approach taken by Great Completion and does not refer at all to Great Completion being a "natural" practice or its being connected with a "natural reality" or any of the many other, incorrect meanings that arise from the mistaken translation "natural Great Completion".

Not stopped, Tib. ma 'gags pa: An important path term in the teaching of both Mahāmudrā and Great Completion. There are two ways to explain this term: theoretically and from a practice perspective. The following explanation is of the latter type. The core of mind has two parts—emptiness and luminosity—are in fact unified so must come that way in practice. However, a practitioner who is still on the path will fall into one extreme or the other and that is called "stoppage". When emptiness and luminosity are unified in practice, there is no stoppage of falling into one extreme or the other. Thus "non-stopped luminosity" is a term that indicates that there is the luminosity with all of its appearance yet that luminosity, for the practitioner, is not mistaken, is not stopped off. "Stopped luminosity" is an experience like luminosity but in which the appearances have, at least to some extent, not been mixed with emptiness.

Output, Tib. gdangs: A general Tibetan term meaning that which is given off by something, for example, the sound that comes from a loudspeaker. In Mahāmudrā and Great Completion, it is the general term used to refer to what is given off by the emptiness factor of the essence of mind. Emptiness is the empty condition of the essence of mind, like space. However, that emptiness has liveliness and liveliness comes off it as compassion and all the other qualities of enlightened mind, and, equally, all the apparatus of dualistic mind. All of this collectively is called its offput. Note that the Great Completion teachings have a special word that is a more refined version of this term; see under complexion.

Poisons, Tib. dug: In Buddhism, poison is a general term for the afflictions. For samsaric beings, the afflictions are poisonous things which harm them. The Buddha most commonly spoke of the three poisons, which are the principal afflictions of desire, aggression, and ignorance. He also spoke of "the five poisons" which is a slightly longer enumeration of the principal afflictions: desire, aggression, delusion, pride, and jealousy.

Post-attainment, Tib. rjes thob: See under equipoise and post-attainment.

Prajna, Skt. prajñā, Tib. shes rab: A Sanskrit term for the type of mind that makes good and precise distinctions between this and that and hence which arrives at correct understanding. It has been translated as "wisdom" but that is not correct because it is, generally speaking, a mental event belonging to dualistic mind where "wisdom" is used to refer to the non-dualistic knower of a buddha. Moreover, the main feature of prajñā is its ability to distinguish correctly between one thing and another and hence to arrive at a correct understanding.

Preserve, Tib. skyong ba: An important term in both Mahāmudrā and Great Completion. In general, it means to defend, protect, nurture, maintain. In the higher tantras it means to keep something just as it is, to nurture that something so that it stays and is not lost. Also, in the higher tantras, it is often used in reference to preserving the state where the state is some particular state of being. Because of this, the phrase "preserve the state" is an important instruction in the higher tantras.

Proliferation, Tib. 'phro ba: A term meaning that the dualistic mind has become active and is giving off thoughts. This is actually the same word as "elaboration" but is the intransitive sense.

Rational mind, Tib. blo: The Kagyu and Nyingma traditions use this term pejoratively for the most part. In the Great Completion and Mahāmudrā teachings, this term specifically means the dualistic mind. It is the villain, so to speak, which needs to be removed from the equation in order to obtain enlightenment. This term is commonly translated simply as mind but that causes confusion with the many other words that are also translated simply as mind. It is not just another mind but is specifically the sort of mind that creates the situation of this and that (ratio in Latin) and hence upholds the duality of saṃsāra. It is the very opposite of the essence of mind. Thus, this is a key term which should be noted and not just glossed over as "mind".

Realization, Tib. rtogs pa: Realization has a very specific meaning which is not always well understood. It refers to correct knowledge that has been gained in such a way that the knowledge does not abate. There are two important points here. Firstly, realization is not absolute. It refers to the removal of obscurations, one at a time. Each time that a practitioner removes an obscuration, he gains a realization because of it. Therefore, there are as many levels of obscuration as there are obscurations. Maitreya, in the *Ornament of Manifest Realizations*, shows how the removal of the various obscurations that go with each of the three realms of samsaric existence produces realization.

Secondly, realization is stable or, as the Tibetan wording says, "unchanging". As Guru Rinpoche pointed out, "Intellectual knowledge is like a patch, it drops away; experiences on the path are temporary, they evaporate like mist; realization is unchanging".

Rigpa, Tib. rig pa: This is the singularly most important term in the whole of Great Completion and Mahāmudrā. In particular, it is the key word of all words in the Great Completion system of the Thorough Cut. Rigpa literally means to know in the sense of "I see!" It is used at all levels of meaning from the coarsest everyday sense of knowing something to the deepest sense of knowing something as presented in the system of Thorough Cut. The system of Thorough Cut uses this term in a very special sense, though it still retains its basic meaning of "to know". To translate it as "awareness", which is common practice today, is a poor practice; there are many kinds of awareness but there is only one rigpa and besides, rigpa is substantially more than just awareness. Since this is such an important term and since it lacks an equivalent in English, I choose not to translate it.

This is the term used to indicate enlightened mind as experienced by the practitioner on the path of these practices. The term itself specifically refers to the dynamic knowing quality of mind. It absolutely does not mean a simple registering, as implied by the word "awareness" which unfortunately is often used to translate this term. There is no word in English that exactly matches it, though the idea of "seeing" or "insight on the spot" is very close. Proof of this is found in the fact that the original Sanskrit term "vidyā" is actually the root of all words in English that start with "vid" and mean "to see", for example, "video", "vision", and so on. Chogyam Trungpa Rinpoche, who was particular skilled at getting Tibetan words into English, also stated that this term rigpa really did not have a good equivalent in English, though he thought that "insight" was the closest. My own conclusion after hearing extensive teaching on it is that rigpa is just best left untranslated. Note that rigpa has both noun and verb forms. To get the verb form, I use "rigpa'ing".

Samsara, Skt. saṃsāra, Tib. 'khor ba: The type of existence that sentient beings have which is that they continue on from one existence to another, always within the enclosure of births that are produced by ignorance and experienced as unsatisfactory. The original Sanskrit means to be constantly going about, here and there. The Tibetan term literally means "cycling", because of which it is frequently translated into English with "cyclic existence" though that is not quite the meaning of the term.

Shamatha, Skt. śhamatha, Tib. gzhi gnas: The name of one of the two main practices of meditation used in the Buddhist system to gain insight into reality. This practice creates a foundation of one-pointedness of mind which can then be used to focus the insight of the other practice, vipaśhyanā. If the development of śhamatha is taken through to completion, the result is a mind that sits stably on its object without any effort and a body which is filled with ease. Altogether, this result of the practice is called "the creation of workability of body and mind".

Shifting events, Tib. yo lang: This refers to the events of a practitioner's life being seen as the shifting events of the dharmakāya. The dharmakāya has an outpouring of display which comes out not as a nice, rationally-ordered experience but as the random and higgledy-piggledy events experienced by the practitioner of that state.

Shine forth, shining forth, Tib. shar ba: This term means "to dawn" or "to come forth into visibility". It is used in Great Completion texts to refer to the particular situation of something coming forth into visibility in mind. There are other words in English like "to appear" that might seem easier to read but they do not catch the attention as this term does in Tibetan and English, both, and indicate that this specific meaning is intended. There will be many times where its specific meaning of something occurring in mind is crucial to a full understanding the text. For example, "shining-forth liberation" means that some content of mind, such as a thought, comes forth and that, on coming forth, is liberated there in mind.

State, Tib. ngang: A key term in Mahāmudrā and Great Completion. Unfortunately it is often not translated and in so doing much meaning is lost. Alternatively, it is often translated as "within" which is incorrect. The term means a "state". A state is a certain, ongoing situation. In Buddhist meditation in general, there are various states that a practitioner has to enter and remain in as part of developing the meditation.

Stoppageless, Tib. 'gag pa med pa: A key term in Mahāmudrā and Great Completion. It is usually translated as "unceasing" but this is a different verb. It refers to the situation in which one thing is not being stopped by another thing. It means "not stopped", "without stoppage", "not blocked and prevented by something else" that is, stoppageless. The verb form associated with it is "not stopped" *q.v.* It is used in relation to the practice of luminosity. A stoppageless luminosity is the actual state of reality and what the practitioner has to aim for. At the beginning of the practice, a practitioner's experience of luminosity will usually not be stoppageless but with stoppages.

Stopped, Tib. 'gags pa: See under not stopped and stoppageless.

Superfactual, Skt. paramārtha,Tib. don dam: This term is paired with the term "fictional" *q.v.* Until now these two terms have been translated as "relative" and "absolute" but those translations are nothing like the original terms. These terms are extremely important in the Buddhist teaching so it is very important that their translations be corrected but, more than that, if the actual meaning of these terms is not presented, the teaching connected with them cannot be understood.

The Sanskrit term literally means "a superior or holy kind of fact" and refers to the wisdom mind possessed by those who have developed themselves spiritually to the point of having transcended saṃsāra. That wisdom is *superior* to an ordinary, un-developed person's consciousness and the *facts* that appear on its surface are superior compared to the facts that appear on the ordinary person's consciousness. Therefore, it is superfact or the holy fact, more literally. What this wisdom knows is true for the beings who have it, therefore what the wisdom sees is superfactual truth.

Superfactual truth, Skt. paramārthasatya, Tib. don dam bden pa: See under superfactual.

Temporary experience, Tib. nyams: The practice of meditation brings with it various experiences that happen simply because of the meditation. These experiences are temporary experiences and not the final, unchanging experience, of realization.

Thorough Cut, Tib. khregs chod: See the introduction for an explanation.

Transparency, Tib. zang thal: This term belongs to the unique vocabulary of Great Completion. It has two connotations: that something is seen directly, in direct perception; and that it is seen with full visibility because there is no agent obscuring the view of it. The term is used to indicate that rigpa is truly present for the practitioner. Luminosity when it is the rigpa of the enlightened side and not the not-rigpa, usually translated as ignorance, of the samsaric side, has transparency or, we could say, full visibility, as one of its qualities precisely because it has none of the factors of mind as such in it, which would obscure it. Transparency means that the rigpa is in full view: it really is rigpa seen in direct perception and it is without rational mind so it is seen without any of the obscuring factors that would make it less than immediately and fully visible.

Unaltered or uncontrived, Tib. ma bcos pa: The opposite of "altered" and "contrived". Something which has not been altered from its native state; something which has been left just as it is.

Un-outflowed, Skt. aśhrāva, Tib. zag pa med pa: Un-outflowed dharmas are ones that are connected with wisdom that has not lost its footing and leaked out into a defiled state; it is self-contained wisdom without any taint of dualistic mind and its apparatus. See also under outflowed.

Upadesha, Skt. upadeśha, Tib. man ngag: See under foremost instruction.

Vipashyana, Skt. vipaśhyanā, Tib. lhag mthong: The Sanskrit name for one of the two main practices of meditation needed in the Buddhist system for gaining insight into reality. The other one, śhamatha, keeps the mind focussed while this one, vipaśhyanā, looks piercingly into the nature of things.

Wisdom, Skt. jñāna, Tib. ye shes: This is a fruition term that refers to the kind of mind, the kind of knower possessed by a buddha. Sentient beings do have this kind of knower but it is covered over by a very complex apparatus for knowing, dualistic mind. If they practise the path to buddhahood, they will leave behind their obscuration and return to having this kind of knower.

The Sanskrit term has the sense of knowing in the most simple and immediate way. This sort of knowing is present at the core of every being's mind. Therefore, the Tibetans called it "the particular type of awareness which is there primordially". Because of their wording, it is often called "primordial wisdom" in English translations but that is too much. It is just wisdom in the sense of the most fundamental knowing possible.

SUPPORTS FOR STUDY

I have been encouraged over the years by all of my teachers and gurus to pass on some of the knowledge I have accumulated in a lifetime dedicated to the study and practice, primarily through the Tibetan Buddhist tradition, of Buddhism. On the one hand they have encouraged me to teach. On the other hand, they are concerned that, while many general books on Buddhism have been and are being published, there are few books that present the actual texts of the tradition. They and many other, closely involved people have encouraged me to make and publish high quality translations of individual texts of the tradition.

The author of the text presented in this book is one of the very important figures in the present-day transmission of the Great Completion teachings in Tibet; the importance of his text for those studying the Three Lines teaching has been explained in the introduction. We have published many texts on the Three Lines teaching, each one carefully selected for its particular treatment of the subject. If you are studying *Feature of the Expert Glorious King* by Patrul Rinpoche you should, in my opinion, also read our translation of Patrul's text and commentary and Dodrupchen Tenpa'i Nyima's *About the Three Lines*. Other publications of ours which concern the practice of

Thorough Cut and are good supports for this kind of study are: *Alchemy of Accomplishment* by Dudjom Jigdrel Yeshe Dorje; *Essential Points of Practice* by Zhechen Gyaltshab; *Way of the Old Dogs* and *Method of Preserving the Face of Rigpa* by Ju Mipham Namgyal; *Peak Doorways to Emancipation* by Shakya Shri; *Hinting at Dzogchen* by Tony Duff; and other titles which are being added all the time.

This text does not present Direct Crossing. For that part of the teaching, there are our publications *Key Points of Direct Crossing called Nectar of the Pure Part* by Khenchen Padma Namgyal and Jigmey Lingpa's most important text *Wisdom Guru, a Guidebook to the Stages of the Path of the Primordial Guardian According to Longchen Nyingthig Great Completion*.

It has also been a project of ours to make tools that non-Tibetans and Tibetans alike could use for the study and translation of Tibetan texts. We prepare electronic editions of Tibetan texts in the Tibetan Text input office of the Padma Karpo Translation Committee and make them available, many for free. We also provide an advanced Reader to go with them, for free. A key feature of our software is that a Tibetan term in a text can be looked up immediately in any of our electronic dictionaries. We suggest the *Illuminator Tibetan-English Dictionary* as the best dictionary for the purpose. For those needing a Tibetan word-processor and pecha-maker, our TibetDoc software and our highest quality typefaces have for many years been the prime resources of Tibetan Buddhist centres throughout the world. The software and texts can be obtained from our web-site whose address is on the copyright page of this book.

TIBETAN TEXT

༄༅། །ཚིག་གསུམ་གནད་དུ་བརྡེག་པའི་ཟིན་བྲིས་དཔལ་ལྡན་བླ་མ་
དམ་པ་གང་གི་ཞལ་ལུང་རྣམས་གང་ཟིན་ཕྱོགས་གཅིག་ཏུ་
བསྡུས་པ་ཆོས་སྐུའི་རིང་བསྲེལ་བཞུགས།།

༄༅། །དེ་ལ་འདིར་མཁས་པ་ཤྲཱི་རྒྱལ་པོའི་ཁྱད་ཆོས་ཚིག་གསུམ་གནད་བརྡེག་གི་ཚིག་གང་ཟིན་རྣམས་ཕྱོགས་གཅིག་བསྡུས་པ་ལ། ཐོག་མར་དགེ་བ་ཀླད་ཀྱི་དོན། བར་དུ་དགེ་བ་གཞུང་གི་དོན། ཐ་མར་དགེ་བ་མཇུག་གི་དོན་དང་གསུམ་ལས། དང་པོ་ནི། བླ་མ་ལ་ཕྱག་འཚལ་ལོ། །ཞེས་དེའང་རྫོགས་ཆེན་རིག་པ་ངོ་སྤྲོད་ཐབས་ལ། ཐོས་བསམ་ལྟ་བའི་ལུགས་དང་། མན་ངག་སྒོམ་པའི་ལུགས། བྱིན་རླབས་འཕོ་བའི་ལུགས་དང་གསུམ་ཡོད་པ་ལས། འདིར་ཕྱི་མ་ལྟར་ཡིན། དེའང་བླ་མ་དུས་གསུམ་སངས་རྒྱས་ཀུན་འདུས་ཀྱི་ངོ་བོར་ཤེས་ཏེ། དད་མོས་ཡིད་ཆེས་དྲག་པོས་དབང་བཞི་བླངས། ཐུགས་ཡིད་བསྲེ་བ་ལ་བརྟེན་ནས། བླ་མའི་དགོངས་རྒྱུད་ཀྱི་རྟོགས་པ་རང་རྒྱུད་ལ་འཕོ་བའི་ཐབས་ལ་བརྩོན་པ་དེ་ཡིན། གཞན་ཡང་དུས་གསུམ་སངས་རྒྱས་རྣམས་ཀྱི་ཐུགས་རྗེ་དང་བྱིན་རླབས་ཇི་ལྟར་མྱུར་ཡང་། ད་ལྟའི་བླ་མ་དགེ་བའི་བཤེས་གཉེན་འདི་ལ་མ་བརྟེན་ན།

རྫོགས་པ་ཆེན་པོའི་མན་ངག་ཟབ་མོ་རྫོགས་པའི་ཐབས་མེད་པ་ཡིན། མཚོན་བྱེད་དཔེའི་བླ་མ་གཟུགས་སྐུ་ཞལ་ཕྱག་གི་རྣམ་པ་ཅན་གྱི་ངོ་བོར་ཤར་ནས། དབང་བསྐུར། རྒྱུད་བཤད། མན་ངག་གནང་པའི་བླ་མ་དང་། ཁྱད་པར་དུ་རང་ལ་ཡེ་ནས་གནས་པའི་གཉུག་མ་དོན་དམ་བྱང་ཆུབ་སེམས་ཀྱི་ཡེ་ཤེས་དེ་ཉིད་ཀྱི་ངོ་བོ་མ་བཅོས་རྗེན་པར་སྟོན་པའི་བླ་མ་དེ་ནི་བཀའ་དྲིན་གསུམ་ལྡན་གྱི་བླ་མ༷་ཡིན་པས་ན་དེ་ལ༷་ཕྱག༷་འཚལ༷་ལོ༷། །དེ་བཞིན་དུ་མཚོན་བྱ་དོན་གྱི་བླ་མ་རང་གི་སྙིང་དབུས་སུ་བཞུགས་པའི་ཆོས་ཉིད་འོད་གསལ་བའི་ཡེ་ཤེས་དེ་ཉིད་བླ་མའི་མན་ངག་གིས་སད་པར་བྱས་པ་དེ་ནི་སྐྱེ་མེད་དོན་གྱི་བླ་མ་ཡིན་པས་ན། དེ་ཉིད་མངོན་དུ་གྱུར་ནས་ཉམས་སུ་བླང་བ་ལ་རབ་ལྟ་བ་མཇལ་བའི་ཕྱག་ཅེས་བྱའོ།། ༄ གཉིས་པ་གཞུང་དོན་ལ། མདོར་བསྟན་པ་དང་། རྒྱས་པར་བཤད་པ་གཉིས། དང་པོ་ལ་དངོས་དང་ཞར་བྱུང་གང་ཟག་སྐལ་བ་དང་ལྡན་པའི་ཕན་ཡོན་བསྟན་པ་གཉིས་ལས། དང་པོ་ནི། ལྟ་བ་ཀློང་ཆེན་རབ་འབྱམས་ཡིན། །སྒོམ་པ་མཁྱེན་བརྩེའི་འོད་ཟེར་ཡིན། །སྤྱོད་པ་རྒྱལ་བའི་མྱུ་གུ་ཡིན། །དེའང་སྤྱིར་ཉེ་ལམ་འོད་གསལ་རྫོགས་པ་ཆེན་པོ་ལ་བརྟེན་པའི་གང་ཟག་དེ་ཚེ་ལུས་གཅིག་ལ་སངས་རྒྱས་པའི་ཐབས་ལ། ལྟ་བ་དང་། སྒོམ་པ། སྤྱོད་པ་གསུམ་ཡ་མ་བྲལ་བ་ཞིག་གི་སྟེང་ནས་མཐར་ཕྱུག་གི་འབྲས་བུ་མངོན་དུ་གྱུར་དགོས་པ་ཡིན། དེ་ཕྱིར་ལྟ་སྒོམ་སྤྱོད་གསུམ་དེ་ཉེ་རྒྱུད་ཀྱི་བརྒྱུད་པའི་བླ་མ་གསུམ་གྱི་མཚན་དོན་དང་སྦྱར་ནས་འཆད་པ་ནི། དེའང་ལྟ་བ༷་ཞེས་བྱ་བ་དེ་ཇི་འདྲ་བ་ཞིག་དགོས་ཞེ་ན། འཁོར་འདས་ཀྱི་ཆོས་ཐམས་ཅད་རིག་སྟོང་ཐིག་ལེ་ཉག་གཅིག་གི་ཀློང་དུ་ཞུབ་ཀྱིས་འདུས་ཤིང་ཡོངས་སུ་ཆུབ་པ་ལྟ་བུའི་ཀློང་ཆེན༷་པོ་ཞིག་ཡིན་པ་དང་། དེ་ལྟ་བུའི་ལྟ་བ་ཀློང་ཆེན་པོ་དེའི་རྩལ་ལས་ཤར་བའི་འཁོར་འདས་ཀྱི་སྣང་བ་རབ༷་འབྱམས༷་མུ་མེད་པ་འདི་དག་མ་འགགས་པར་གསལ་ལ་མ་འདྲེས་པར་ཤར་བ་དང་། ཤར་ཀྱང་འཁོར་འདས་ཐམས་ཅད་རིག་པ་ཆོས་

ཉིད་མཉམ་པ་ཆེན་པོའི་ཀློང་ལས་གཡོ་མ་མྱོང་བ་ཡིན་ནོ། །དེ་ཉིད་ཉམས་སུ་བླངས་ཏེ། སྒོམ་པ་ཞེས་པ་དེ་ཇི་ལྟ་བུ་ཞིག་དགོས་ཞེ་ན། ཆོས་ཐམས་ཅད་ཀྱི་གནས་ལུགས་དོན་དམ་བྱང་ཆུབ་ཀྱི་སེམས་ཆོས་སྐུ་ཆེན་པོ་དེ་ཉིད་ཀྱི་དོན་ཇི་ལྟ་བ་བཞིན་མ་ནོར་བར་མཁྱེན་པའི་མཁྱེན་པ་དང་། དེ་ལྟར་མ་རྟོགས་པའི་སེམས་ཅན་རྣམས་ལ་བརྩེ་བའི་སྙིང་རྗེ་ཆེན་པོ་རྩོལ་མེད་དུ་འབྱུང་བ་གཉིས་ཟུང་དུ་འཇུག་པ་གཉིས་ངེས་པར་དུ་དགོས། དེས་ན་དེ་ལྟ་བུའི་ཇི་ལྟ་མཁྱེན་པའི་ཡེ་ཤེས་རིག་ངོ་ལྷག་གེར་མཐོང་བའི་ལྷག་མཐོང་ཉི་མ་ལྟ་བུ་དང་། ཇི་སྙེད་པའི་འགྲོ་བ་ཡོངས་ལ་དམིགས་པ་མེད་པའི་བརྩེ་བའི་སྙིང་རྗེ་ཆེན་པོ་ཉི་མའི་འོད་ཟེར་དང་ཆོས་མཚུངས་པ་གཉིས་ཟུང་དུ་འཇུག་པའི་སྒོམ་པ་དེ་ལ་སྒོམ་པ་མཁྱེན་བརྩེའི་འོད་ཟེར་ཡིན་ཞེས་སོ། །དེ་བཞིན་དུ་ལྟ་སྒོམ་སྤྱོད་གསུམ་ཡ་མ་བྲལ་བའི་སྤྱོད་པ་དེ་ཇི་འདྲ་ཞིག་ཡིན་ཞེ་ན། སྤྱོད་པ་རྒྱལ་བའི་མྱུ་གུ་ཡིན་ཞེས་དཔེར་ན་མྱུ་གུ་ལས་སྡོང་པོ་དང་ལོ་མ་དང་འབྲས་བུ་སོགས་རྒྱ་ཆེན་པོ་འབྱུང་བ་བཞིན། རྒྱལ་བའི་སྲས་པོ་མྱུ་གུ་ལྟ་བུའི་བྱང་ཆུབ་སེམས་དཔའི་ཕྱིན་དྲུག་གི་ལམ་ལ་བསླབས་ན་སྡོང་པོ་དང་། ལོ་མ་འབྲས་བུ་ལྟ་བུའི་བྱང་ཆུབ་ཕྱོགས་ཀྱི་འབྲས་བུའི་ཆོས་སྐུ་བཞི་ཡེ་ཤེས་ལྔ་སོགས་རང་བྱུང་རྩོལ་མེད་ལྷུན་གྲུབ་ཀྱི་ཚུལ་གྱིས་འབྱུང་བས་ནའོ། །ཕྱིར་མཉམ་བཞག་གི་རིག་ངོ་ལ་ཚོགས་ཆེན་ཡེ་རྫོགས་ཆེན་པོ་ཡིན་པས་ཕྱིན་དྲུག་གི་ཡོན་ཏན་ཐམས་ཅད་རང་ཆས་སུ་རྫོགས་པ་ནི། གང་དུ་མི་འཛིན་པ་སྦྱིན་པ། གང་ལ་མ་ཆགས་པ་ཚུལ་ཁྲིམས། གང་ལ་མི་སྐྲག་པ་བཟོད་པ། མི་བརྩོན་པ་བརྩོན་འགྲུས། རིག་པ་རང་བབས་སུ་གནས་པ་བསམ་གཏན། རིག་པ་རང་བྱུང་གི་ཤེས་རབ་དང་དྲུག་རང་ལ་རྫོགས་པའོ། །དེའི་སྟོབས་ཀྱིས་རྗེས་ཐོབ་སྤྱོད་ལམ་གྱི་སྐབས་སུ་ཕྱིན་དྲུག་རང་ཤུགས་ཀྱིས་འབྱུང་བས་ན་རྒྱལ་བའི་མྱུ་གུ་བྱང་ཆུབ་སེམས་དཔའི་སྤྱོད་པ་ཐམས་ཅད་རིག་པ་ཡེ་ཤེས་ཆེན་པོའི་གྲོགས་ཡིན་ནོ། །དེ་ལྟར་ལྟ་སྒོམ་སྤྱོད་གསུམ་དེ། བརྒྱུད་གསུམ་

བླ་མའི་མཚན་དང་སྦྱར་ནས་རྒྱལ་བ་དགོངས་བརྒྱུད་ཀློང་ཆེན་རབ་འབྱམས། རིག་འཛིན་བརྡ་བརྒྱུད་འཇིགས་མེད་གླིང་པ། གང་ཟག་སྙན་བརྒྱུད་རྒྱལ་བའི་མྱུ་གུ་དང་སྦྱར་ཚུལ་གཡུ་ཁོག་བྱ་བྲལ་གྱི་ཟིན་བྲིས་སུ་གསལ། གཞན་ཡང་བླ་མ་དམ་པའི་ཞལ་རྒྱུན་ལྟར་ན། ལྟ་སྒོམ་སྤྱོད་གསུམ་གྱི་བླ་མ་གསུམ་དེའི་ངོ་བོ་ལ་སྦྱར་ཏེ། དཔེར་ན་ལྟ་བ་ནི། འཕགས་པའི་ཡུལ་ན་དགའ་རབ་རྡོ་རྗེ་དང་། བོད་ཀྱི་ཡུལ་དུ་ཀློང་ཆེན་རབ་འབྱམས་གཉིས་ཀྱི་ལྟ་བ་ལྟ་བུ་ཞེས་ལྟ་བ་ཐམས་ཅད་ཀྱི་ཡང་རྩེ་ཡིན་པ་དང་། སྒོམ་པ་ནི། འཇིགས་མེད་གླིང་པ་ལྟ་བུ་ཞེས། ཉིན་མཚན་གཡེལ་བ་མེད་པར་སྒོམ་པས་བསྒོམ་བྱུང་ཤེས་རབ་ཀྱི་ཀློང་རྡོལ་ཏེ། རིག་པའི་གནས་ལྔ་སོགས་ལ་མ་བསླབས་ཀྱང་ཆགས་ཐོགས་མེད་པར་མཁྱེན་པ་དེ། ཁོ་བོའི་མཉམ་པར་བཞག་པའི་ཁྱད་ཆོས་ཡིན་གསུངས་པ་ལྟར་ལགས། སྤྱོད་པ་ནི་ཛ་ཁྲ་མ་བླ་མ་ལྟ་བུ་ཞེས། སྐུ་ཚེ་དེ་ལ་ཉེས་ལྟུང་ཕྲ་མོས་ཀྱང་མ་གོས་པར། རྒྱལ་སྲས་ཀྱི་སྤྱོད་པའི་ཕ་རོལ་ཏུ་སོན་པ་ལྟ་བུ་ཡིན་པས་ན་བླ་མ་དེ་གསུམ་ལ་སྦྱར་བའང་ཡིན་ནོ།།

༈ གཉིས་པ་ཞར་བྱུང་གང་ཟག་སྐལ་བ་དང་ལྡན་པའི་ཕན་ཡོན་བསྟན་པ་ནི། དེ་ལྟར་ཉམས་སུ་ལེན་པ་ལ། །ཚེ་གཅིག་སངས་རྒྱས་ལ་ཐང་མེད། །མིན་ཀྱང་བློ་བདེ་ཨ་ལ་ལ། །ཞེས་དེ་ལྟར་འཇིག་རྟེན་ཚེ་འདིའི་བྱ་བཞག་ཐམས་ཅད་བློས་བཏང་སྟེ་དབེན་པའི་རི་ཁྲོད་བསྟེན་ནས་ལྟ་སྒོམ་སྤྱོད་གསུམ་ཡ་མ་བྲལ་བར་རྩེ་གཅིག་ཏུ་ཉམས་སུ་ལེན་པ་ལ་ནི། བརྩོན་འགྲུས་རབ་དང་། དད་པ་རབ་ཅིག་ཡོད་པའི་ལས་འཕྲོ་ལྡན་པའི་སྐལ་ལྡན་ཡིན་ན། མི་ཚེ་གཅིག་པོ་འདི་ལ་ཀ་དག་གཞི་ཐོག་ཏུ་གྲོལ་ནས་སངས་རྒྱས་པ་ལ་ཐང་མེད་པ་ཞིག་ཡིན། འོན་ཀྱང་སླེབས་དུས་འདིར། རང་ཅག་ལ་དད་པ་དང་མོས་གུས་སྙིང་རྗེ་ཆུང་བ་དང་། བརྩོན་པ་དང་སྙིང་རུས་ཞན་སྟབས་ཆོས་འདི་ཉམས་སུ་བླང་ཚད་ཚེ་འདིར་གྲོལ་ངེས་ཡིན་ཞེས་ཁ་ཆོན་ཆོད་དགའ་ནའང་། མིན་ཀྱང་བློ་བདེ་ཨ་ལ་ལ་ཞེས།

དེ་ལྟར་མིན༷་ཀྱང་ཆོས་འདི་ཉམས་སུ་བླང་བའི་རྣལ་འབྱོར་པ་དེ་ཀུ་ཡངས་ཀློ་
བདེ༷་བའི་ངང་ནས་ཚེ་འདིར་གང་སྣང་ལམ་དུ་ཁྱེར་ཤེས་པ་འཁྲུལ་སྣང་ལ་ཞེན་
ཆགས་མེད་པ་དང་། སྲིད་པ་རྒྱལ་པོ་བྱེད་པ། ཚེ་ཕྱི་མའང་ཇི་ལྟར་ཞན་
ཡང་རང་བཞིན་སྤྲུལ་བའི་ཞིང་གང་རུང་ཞིག་གི་མན་ལ་གནས་མི་དགོས་པས་
ན་ཨུ༷་ལུ༷་ལུ༷་ཞེས་མན་ངག་འདི་ཉམས་སུ་ལེན་པ་ལ་སྤྲོ་བ་བསྐྱེད་པའོ།།
༄ གཉིས་པ་གཞུང་དོན་རྒྱས་པར་བཤད་པ་ལ། ལྟ་སྒོམ་སྤྱོད་
གསུམ་ལས། དང་པོ་ལྟ་བ་རྒྱས་པར་བཤད་པ་ལ། ངོ་རང་ཐོག་ཏུ་སྤྲད་
པ་དང་། ཐག་གཅིག་ཐོག་ཏུ་བཅད་པ། གདེངས་གྲོལ་ཐོག་ཏུ་བཅའ་བ་
གསུམ་ལས། དང་པོ་ནི། ལྟ་བ་ཀློང་ཆེན་རབ་འབྱམས་ནི། །ཚིག་
གསུམ་དོན་གྱི་གནད་དུ་བརྡེག །དང་པོ་རང་སེམས་ལྷོད་དེ་བཞག །མི་
སྤྲོ་མི་བསྡུ་རྣམ་རྟོག་མེད། །ངང་ལ་ཁྱུམ་གནས་ལྷོད་དེའི་དུས། །ཐོལ་
བྱུང་བློ་རྟེག་ཕཊ་ཅིག་བརྒྱབ། །དྲག་ལ་ངར་ཐུང་ཨེ་མ་ཧོ། །ཅི་ཡང་མ་
ཡིན་ཧད་དེ་བ། །ཧད་དེ་བ་ལ་ཟང་ཐལ་ལེ། །ཟང་མ་ཐལ་བྱུང་བརྗོད་དུ་
མེད། །ཆོས་སྐུའི་རིག་པ་ངོས་ཟུངས་ཤིག །ངོ་རང་ཐོག་ཏུ་སྤྲད་པ་སྟེ་
གནད་དང་པོའོ། །ཞེས་དེའང་ལྟ༷་བ༷་ཀློང༷་ཆེན༷་རབ༷་འབྱམས༷་ཞེས་བྱ་བ་ནི༷་
འདི་ལྟ་སྟེ། ངོ་རང་ཐོག་ཏུ་སྤྲད་པ། ཐག་གཅིག་ཐོག་ཏུ་བཅད་པ།
གདེང་གྲོལ་ཐོག་ཏུ་བཅའ་བ་སྟེ་ཚིགས༷་གསུམ༷་དོན༷་གྱི༷་གདམས་ངག་གི་ཉམས་
ལེན་གནད༷་དུ་བརྡེ༷ག༷་པ་ལ་བརྟེན་ནས་འཁྲུལ་བའི་སྲོག་རྩ་གཅོད་པ་ནི།
དཔེར་ན་ཤན་པ་སྲོག་གཅོད་ཀྱི་གནད་ལ་མཁས་པ་ཞིག་གིས་གང་གསད་བྱ་
དེའི་སྲོག་དེ་མ་ཐག་ཏུ་གཅོད་ནུས་པ་བཞིན་ཚིག་གསུམ་དོན་གྱི་གནད་རྡེག་པའི་
མན་ངག་ལ་མཁས་ན་འཁྲུལ་སྣང་འཁོར་བའི་སྲོག་དེ་མ་ཐག་ཏུ་གཅོད་ནུས་པ་
ཡིན་ནོ། །དེས་ན་ངོ་རང་ཐོག་ཏུ་ཇི་ལྟར་སྤྲད་དགོས་ཞེ་ན། ཐོག་མར་ལྟ་
བ་ངོ་མ་འཕྲོད་པ་སྤྲོད་པའི་ཐབས་ལ། མཚན་ཉིད་ཐེག་པ་ལྟར་ན། ལྟ་བ་
ལུང་རིགས་ཀྱིས་གཏན་ལ་དབབ་སྟེ། ལུང་གིས་གཏན་ལ་དབབ་པ་ལ།

རྒྱལ་པའི་བཀའ་དང་། རྗེས་འཇུག་གི་བསྟན་བཅོས་ལ་བརྟེན་པ་དང་།
རིགས་པས་གཏན་ལ་ཕབ་ཚུལ། ཤིང་རྟ་རྣམ་བདུན་དང་། རྣམ་ལྔའི་
རིགས་པ་ལྔ་བུ་དང་ཡོད་མེད་སྐྱེ་འགོག་དང་། མཐའ་བཞིའི་སྐྱེ་
འགོག །རྡོ་རྗེ་གཟེགས་མ། གཅིག་དུ་བྲལ་གྱི་རིགས་པ་སོགས་ཀྱིས་
གཏན་ལ་འབེབས་པ་དང་། གསང་སྔགས་ཐུན་མོང་བའི་ལུགས་ལྟར་ན།
དབང་གསུམ་པའི་དཔེའི་ཡེ་ཤེས་ལ་བརྟེན་ནས། བཞི་བས་དོན་གྱི་ཡེ་ཤེས་
ངོ་སྤྲོད་ཚུལ་སོགས་མང་ཡང་། འདིར་ཐུན་མོང་མ་ཡིན་པ་རང་ལུགས་
རྫོགས་པ་ཆེན་པོ་ཡང་གསང་བླ་ན་མེད་པའི་ལུགས་ལྟར་ན། དང་པོ་ལུས་
གཡོ་འགུལ་མེད་པ་རི་བོ་ལྟ་བུར་ལྷོད་ལ་བཞག་ཞབས་དཀྱིལ་ཀྲུང་བྱ།
ལག་གཉིས་སེམས་ཉིད་ངལ་གསོའི་ཕྱག་རྒྱ་བྱ། སྣལ་ཚིགས་དྲང་པོར་
བསྲིངས། མིག་བར་སྣང་ལ་ཧ་རེར་བལྟ། དེ་ནི་ལུས་ཀྱི་བཞག་ཐབས་
ཡིན། སྙིང་ཐིག་སྙན་རྒྱུད་ཤོག་དྲིལ་ཟབ་མོ་ལས། ལུས་དྲང་ན་རྩ་དྲང་།
རྩ་དྲང་ན་རླུང་དྲང་། རླུང་དྲང་ན་སེམས་ལས་སུ་རུང་བའི་དགོས་པ་ཡོད་དོ་
ཞེས་གསུངས། དེ་བཞིན་དུ་ངག་གི་རླུང་ཡང་རང་བབས་སུ་ཁ་ནས་དལ་
བུར་འབྱིན་འཇུག་བྱ་དགོས་ཏེ། ཁ་ནས་ཡེ་ཤེས་ཀྱི་རླུང་རྒྱུ་བ་དང་། སྣ་
ནས་མ་དག་པའི་རླུང་རྒྱུ་བས་རྩ་ཀ་ཏི་ཤེལ་སྦུག་ནང་དུ་རླུང་རན་པར་རྒྱུ་ཚེ་
ལས་རླུང་ཉི་ཁྲི་ཆིག་སྟོང་རང་སར་འགགས་ཏེ་རྟོག་ཚོགས་འཁྲུལ་པའི་སྣང་བ་
ཐམས་ཅད་རང་ཤུགས་ཀྱིས་ཞི་བའི་དགོས་པ་ཡོད་དེ། ལྟ་བ་ནམ་མཁའ་
སྤྲིན་བྲལ་ལས། དབུགས་ནི་འབྱུང་རྔུབ་སོ་ཡི་བར་ནས་བྱེད། །ཀ་ཏི་
ཤེལ་སྦུག་སྙིང་ནས་ཁར་འབྲེལ་གནད། །གནད་ཀྱིས་ལས་རླུང་འགགས་
ཚེ་རྟོག་ཚོགས་ཞི། །ཁྲེགས་ཆོད་ལྟ་བ་རང་གདངས་ཐད་ཀར་འཆར། །
རིག་པ་མངོན་དུ་གྱུར་བའི་མན་ངག་ཡིན། །ཞེས་དང་། གྲུབ་དབང་
ཞབས་དཀར་པས། རླུང་གནད་སྣ་ནས་མི་གཏོང་ཁ་ནས་གཏོང་། །སོ་
དང་མཆུ་གཉིས་བག་ཙམ་མ་རེག་པར། །ཤིན་ཏུ་དལ་བུའི་རླུང་གིས་འབྱིན་

འཇུག་བྱ། །ཞེས་དང་། སྙན་རྒྱུད་ལས། ངག་གི་རླུང་རྩོལ་མེད་རང་བབས་སུ་ཁ་ནས་ཕྱིར་འཇོན་རིང་བ་ཙམ་དུ་བཞག་པས། འགྲོ་འོང་ལས་ཀྱི་རླུང་རང་སར་བཞག་པས་ཀུན་རྟོག་ཉོན་མོངས་པའི་རླུང་རང་དེངས་སུ་སོང་ནས། རིག་པ་ཡེ་ཤེས་ཀྱི་རླུང་དབྱིངས་སུ་འཁྱིལ་བ་ལམ་འདིའི་ཁྱད་ཆོས་ཡིན་ནོ། །ཞེས་སོ། །དེ་ནི་ངག་གི་བཞག་ཐབས་ཡིན། དེ་བཞིན་དུ་སེམས་ཀྱང་མི་གཡོ། མི་བསམ། མི་སྒོམ། བཅས་བཅོས། སྤང་བླང་། དགག་སྒྲུབ་གང་ཡང་མི་བྱེད་པར་དང་པོ་ནས་རང་སེམས་ལྷོད་དེ། ནམ་མཁའ་ལྟ་བུའི་ངང་ལ་རང་སར་བཞག་དགོས། དེ་ལྟར་བཞག་ནས་སེམས་ཀྱི་རྣམ་རྟོག་འཕྲོ་རྒོད་རགས་པ་འདི་དག་དེངས་སུ་མ་བཙུག་ན། སེམས་ཉིད་ཀྱི་རང་ཞལ་མི་མཐོང་བས་ན། དུས་གསུམ་གྱི་འཁྲུལ་རྟོག་རགས་པ་དང་ཕྲ་བའི་ངང་ལ་ཅི་ཡང་མི་བསམ་ལྷོད་དེ་བཞག་པ་འདི་སེམས་ཀྱི་བཞག་ཐབས་རེད། ཨ་འཛོམས་འབྲུག་པ་ཚང་གིས་སློབ་མ་རྣམས་ལ་ལོ་བཞི་ལྔ་རེའི་ཚེ་ལ་འདི་ལྟར་བྱས་ནས་འདུག་ཏུ་བཙུག་པ་ཡིན། བླ་མ་མི་ཕམ་རིན་པོ་ཆེས། འདི་ཡིན་རྒྱུ་ཀུན་གཞི་ཡིན་ཀྱང་འདི་ལྟ་བུ་ལ་མ་བརྟེན་ན་ཡང་དག་པའི་ཡེ་ཤེས་རྒྱུད་ལ་མི་སྐྱེ་གསུངས། འདི་སེམས་ཀྱི་བཞག་ཐབས་ཡིན། ཐབས་དེ་ལ་བརྟེན་ནས་ཐབས་བྱུང་གི་ཡེ་ཤེས་རྟོགས་དགོས། འདིར་རང་ལུགས་རྫོགས་པ་ཆེན་པོའི་བརྒྱུད་གསུམ་བླ་མ་དག་གིས་ཕྱག་བཞེས་ནི། སེམས་རྣམ་རྟོག་གི་འགྱུ་བ་ཐམས་ཅད་རང་སར་ཡལ་ས་ནས་ངོ་སྤྲོད་པ་ཡིན། དེའང་ཕྱི་ཡུལ་གཟུགས་སྒྲ་དྲི་རོ་རེག་བྱ་སྟེ་ཚོགས་དྲུག་གི་ཡུལ་སྣང་གང་ཤར་ཀྱང་དེའི་སྟེང་དུ་རྣམ་པར་རྟོག་པ་ཕར་མི་སྟོ། དེ་བཞིན་དུ་དུག་གསུམ་དུག་ལྔའི་རྟོག་པ་གང་ཤར་ཀྱང་། དེའི་གཉེན་པོ་བརྟེན་ནས་དམིགས་པ་ཚུར་ལ་མི་བསྡུ་བར་ལྷོད་ལ་བཞག་ཆོ། འདས་པའི་རྟོག་པ་འགགས་ནས་མེད། མ་འོངས་པའི་རྟོག་པ་མ་སྐྱེས་ནས་མེད། ད་ལྟའི་རྣམ་པར་རྟོག་པ་རང་ཡལ་སོང་ནས་མེད། དུས་གསུམ་གྱི་རྣམ་རྟོག་མེད་

པར་རང་བབས་མ་བཅོས་པའི་ངང་དུ་མཉམ་པར་བཞག་ནས་འོད་གསལ་བའི་ཡེ་ཤེས་སྐྱེ་དགོས། འོན་ཀྱང་ལས་དང་པོ་བའི་གནས་སྐབས་ན་རྣམ་རྟོག་སྤྲོ་བསྡུ་མེད་པར་རང་བཞག་གཉུག་མའི་ངང་བསྐྱང་ཁྱེལ་བྱུས་ཀྱང་། གནས་ཆ་རྐྱང་པ་ལྟ་བུ་རེ་དང་། བདེ་གསལ་མི་རྟོག་པའི་ཉམས་ཞེན་གྱི་ཤུན་པ་དང་བྲལ་མི་ཐུབ་པས་ན། དེའི་ངང༷་ལ༷་ཕྲུམ༷་སྤེ་གནས༷་པ་ལྟ་བུའི་སྒོ་གསུམ་ལྷོད་དེ༷འི་ངང་དུ་བཞག་པའི་དུས༷་ན། ཉམས་ཞེན་གྱི་ཤུན་པ་དང་། རྣམ་པར་རྟོག་པའི་གོས་རྩུལ་དང་བྲལ་མ་ཐུབ་པར་ཡོད་ན། དེ་དག་དང་བྲལ་ཏེ་རིག་པ་ཟང་ཐལ་རྗེན་པ་གཅེར་བུར་ལྷང་ལ་འབུད་པའི་ཆེད་དུ། ཐོལ༷་བྱུང་ཀློ་རྡེ༷ག་གམ་གློ་བུར་དུ་ཐོག་བབས་པ་ལྟ་བུའི་ཕཊ་ཅིག་བརྒྱབ་དགོས་གསུངས། ཕཊ་སྒྲ་དེའང་དབྱངས་ཅན་དང་སྒྲ་གདངས་རིང་བ། སྐད་མོ་དེ་ལྟ་བུ་མ་ཡིན་པར་ཕཊ་སྒྲ་ཤུགས་དྲག༷་ལ༷་ངར༷་སྒྲ་ཅན། ཡུན་ཐུང་བ་དེ་འདྲ་ཞིག་རྒྱག་དགོས། ཕཊ་སྒྲ་དེའི་རྐྱེན་གྱིས་དུས་གསུམ་གྱི་རྟོག་ཚོགས་དང་ཉམས་ཞེན་གྱི་ཤུན་པ་མཐའ་དག་དང་བྲལ་བའི་རིག་པ་རང་གནས་ཀྱི་ཡེ་ཤེས་དེ་རྗེན་ལ་འབུད་ཐུབ། དེ་འདྲའི་རིག་པ་དེ་ནི་སྐྱེ་མེད་དང་ལས་འགག་མེད་ཟང་ཐལ་གྱི་རིག་ཆ་རྗེན་པ། རྣམ་ཤེས་ཚོགས་བརྒྱད་དང་བྲལ་བའི་ཡེ་ཤེས། སྤུར་མེད་གསར་བྱུང་མ་ཡིན་པར་ཡེ་ནས་རང་དང་འབྲལ་མ་མྱོང་བའི་ལྷན་གཅིག་སྐྱེས་པའི་སེམས་ལས་འདས་པའི་ཡེ་ཤེས་ཡིན་པས་ན། དེ་ནི་དུས་གསུམ་སངས་རྒྱས་ཐམས་ཅད་ཀྱི་མཐར་ཐུག་གི་དགོངས་པ། མ་མཁའ་འགྲོ་འབུམ་གྱི་སྙིང་ཁྲག་ཆོས་ཕུང་བརྒྱད་ཁྲི་བཞི་སྟོང་གི་ཡང་བཅུད་དེ་མ་གབ་རྗེན་པར་ངོ་འཕྲོད་པ་ནི་ཨེ་མ་ཧོ་ཞེས་ངོ་མཚར་བའི་གནས་ལགས་སོ། །དེའི་ཚེ་ན་ཡོད་མེད་ཡིན་མིན་སོགས་ངོས་བཟུང་ཐམས་ཅད་དང་བྲལ་བས་ན་ཅི་ཡང་མ་ཡིན༷་པ་དང་། འདི་ཡིན་གྱི་གཟའ་གཏད་ཐམས་ཅད་དང་བྲལ་བའི་གྲོལ་བ་མངོན་དུ་གྱུར་བ་ལ་ཧད༷་དེ༷་བ༷་ཞེས་བྱའོ། །དབང་དུས་སུ་ངོ་སྤྲོད་ཚུལ་ཡང་འདི་ལྟར་ཡིན། སྒྲ་ཐལ་འགྱུར་རྩ་བའི་རྒྱུད་ཀྱི་ནང་དུ་ངོ་སྤྲོད་

ཐབས་དྲུག་གསུངས་པའི་གཅིག་ཀྱང་འདི་ཡིན། བླ་མས་ཕཊ་སྒྲ་བརྗོད་པ་དང་། ཡང་ན་རང་གིས་རང་ལ་ཕཊ་དྲག་པོ་བརྗོད་ཀྱང་རུང་སྟེ། དེ་ལ་བརྟེན་ནས་དུས་གསུམ་གྱི་རྟོག་ཚོགས་ཐད་ཀྱིས་བཅད་ཚེ། རང་གནས་ཀྱི་ཡེ་ཤེས་མངོན་དུ་གྱུར་བའི་ངོ་བོ་ལ་བལྟ་རྒྱུ་དེ་ཡིན། སྤྱིར་ཧད་དེ་བ་ཞེས་པ་དེ་སེམས་གཏད་སོ་དང་བྲལ་བའི་ཆ་ནས་བརྗོད་པ་དང་། ཟང་ཐལ་ལེ་ཞེས་པ་དེ་ཆགས་ཐོགས་དང་བྲལ་བའི་ཆ་ནས་ཟེར། དེས་ན་ཆགས་ཐོགས་མེད་པ་ཕར་དངོས་པོ་ཐམས་ཅད་ཟིལ་གྱིས་གནོན་ཀྱང་། ཚུར་གང་གིས་ཀྱང་མི་ཚུགས་པའི་རྡོ་རྗེའི་ཆོས་བདུན་དང་ལྡན་པ་ཞིག་ལ་གོ་དགོས། སྐབས་འདིར་སེམས་ཧད༷་དེ༷་བ༷་ཡིན་པ་ལ༷་སྟོང་རྒྱང་དང་སྟོང་པ་ཕྱང་ཆད་དང་། ཧ་ཤང་གི་ལྟ་བ་ལྟ་བུ་མ་ཡིན་པར་སེམས་ལས་འདས་པའི་ཡེ་ཤེས་སྟོང་གསལ་འགག་མེད་ཀྱི་རིག་ཆ་རྗེན་པ་མངོན་དུ་གྱུར་བ་ལ་ཟང༷་ཐལ༷་ལེ༷་ཞེས་གོ་དགོས། དེ་འདྲ་བའི་ཟང༷་མ༷་ཐལ༷་བྱུང༷་གི་རིག་པ་དེ་གཅིག་དང་ཐ་དད། རྟག་དང་མི་རྟག །ཡོད་མེད། ཡིན་མིན། སྐྱེ་འགག་ལ་སོགས་པའི་སྤྲོས་པའི་མཐའ་ཐམས་ཅད་དང་བྲལ་བའི་རིག་པ་ཟང་ཐལ་ཤེལ་གོང་ལྟ་བུའི་རིག་ཆ་རྗེན་པ་དེ་ནི། སྒྲ་དང་ཚིག་གིས་བརྗོད༷་དུ༷་མེད་པ་དང་། ཡིད་ལ་བསམ་དུ་མེ༷ད་པ་ཞིག་ཡིན་པས་ན། སྒྲ་གཅན་འཛིན་གྱི་ཡུམ་བསྟོད་ལས། སྨྲ་བསམ་བརྗོད་མེད་ཤེས་རབ་ཕ་རོལ་ཕྱིན། །མ་སྐྱེས་མི་འགག་ནམ་མཁའི་ངོ་བོ་ཉིད། །སོ་སོ་རང་རིག་ཡེ་ཤེས་སྤྱོད་ཡུལ་བ། །དུས་གསུམ་རྒྱལ་བའི་ཡུམ་ལ་ཕྱག་འཚལ་ལོ། །ཞེས་པ་ལྟར། དུས་གསུམ་གྱི་རྟོག་པ་དང་བྲལ་བའི་སེམས་ཀྱི་གཤིས་ལ་བལྟས་ཚེ་མཐའ་དབུས་ཐམས་ཅད་དང་བྲལ་བའི་རིག་པ་དྭངས་སེང་ངེ་བ་དེ་ལ་ཆོས་སྐུ༷འི་རིག༷་པ༷་ཞེས་ངོས་ཟུང༷ས་ཞིག༷་ཅེས་སོ། །དེའི་ཚུལ་ཡང་། ཧཱུྃ་སྐད་དུ། ད་ལྟའི་ཤེས་རིག་མ་འགགས་སལ་ལེ་བ༔ ཀུན་བཟང་གདོད་མའི་མགོན་པོ་དེ་ག་འོ༔ ཞེས་སོ། །དེ་བཞིན་དུ་སྒོ་གསུམ་མ་བཅོས་ལྷོད་ལ་བཞག་ཚེ་དུས་གསུམ་གྱི་རྟོག

པ་དང་བྲལ་བའི་རིག་པ་སལ་ལེ་སང་ངེ་རྗེན་ལ་བུད་པ་དེ་རྫོགས་པ་ཆེན་པོའི་
ཚིག་བརྒྱའི་མདོ་འགག་དང་། ཁྲེགས་ཆོད་ལྟ་བའི་གནད་འགག་ཡིན་ཏེ།
ཞབས་དཀར་བས། ཁྲེགས་ཆོད་ལྟ་བའི་གནད་འགག་རིག་པ་ནི། །རྗེན་
ལ་ཕུད་ནས་སལ་ལེར་སྐྱོང་བ་ལ། །ཟེར་བའི་གནད་འདི་ཁོ་ན་གལ་ཆེ་
སྟེ། །འདི་ནི་ཚིག་བརྒྱའི་མདོ་འགག་ཡིན་པས་ན། །སྐལ་ལྡན་སྙིང་གི་
བུ་རྣམས་ཤེས་པར་གྱིས། །ཞེས་གསུངས། དེ་ལྟར་སེམས་ལ་བསམ་
བརྗོད་དང་བྲལ་བའི་རང་རིག་རང་གསལ་རང་ཤེས་ཀྱི་རྣམ་པ་ཅན་དེ་རྗེན་པར་
རྟོགས་ན་འདི་ཡིས་འཁོར་འདས་ཡོངས་ལ་ཁྱབ་པས་ན་འདི་ནི་འཁོར་འདས་
ཀུན་ཁྱབ་ཀྱི་ཡེ་ཤེས་ཡིན་པ་དང་དུས་གསུམ་རྒྱལ་བ་ཡོངས་ཀྱི་ཐུགས་ཆོས་
དབྱིངས་ཆེན་པོ་ཡིན་ཏེ། ལང་གྲོ་ལོ་ཙཱ་བའི་ཞལ་ནས། སེམས་ལ་
བསམ་དུ་མེད་པའི་ཉམས། །རང་གསལ་རྗེན་པར་གནས་པ་འདི། །
འཁོར་འདས་ཀུན་ལ་ཁྱབ་པ་ཉིད། །དུས་གསུམ་རྒྱལ་བའི་དགོངས་པ་
ལགས། །ཞེས་སོ། །དེ་ལྟར་རང་གི་སེམས་ལ་རྣམ་པར་རྟོག་པ་ཇི་ལྟར་
འགྱུ་ཡང་འགྱུ་བཞིན་དུ་སྟོང་པ་ཐད་ཀའི་ནམ་མཁའ་ལ་བསེར་བུ་རྒྱུ་བ་ལྟ་བུ།
སེམས་ཉིད་སྟོང་པ་ཟང་ཐལ་རྗེན་པའི་ངོ་བོ་ལ་ཁོ་ཐག་ཆོད་ན་དེ་ལས་གཞན་
མེད་དེ། མི་ཕམ་རིན་པོ་ཆེས། དེ་ཚེ་ཐད་ཀའི་ནམ་མཁའ་ལ། །
བལྟས་པ་བཞིན་དུ་རང་གི་སེམས། །འགྱུ་བཞིན་པ་ལ་སྟོང་པ་ཉིད། །
ངེས་ཤེས་ཁོ་ཐག་ཆོད་པ་དགོས། །ཞེས་གསུངས། དེ་སྔ་ཡན་ལ་རང་
ཅག་གི་ཁ་ཕར་བལྟས་འཁྲུལ་བའི་དབང་དུ་སོང་ནས་དོན་གྱི་གནས་ལུགས་
མཐོང་མ་ནུས་པ་ཡིན་ཀྱང་། ད་ནི་ཁ་ཚུར་བལྟས་ཏེ་སེམས་ཀྱིས་སེམས་ལ་
ལྟོས་དང་། སེམས་སྟོང་པ་མཐའ་དབུས་ཐམས་ཅད་དང་བྲལ་བའི་བཞི་ཆ་
གསུམ་བྲལ་གྱི་རིག་པ་རྗེན་སེང་ངེ་བ་དེ་མངོན་དུ་གྱུར་པ། དེ་ལ་ཆོས་སྐུའི་
རིག་པ་ཞེས་བརྗོད་པ་ཡིན་ཏེ། མི་ཕམ་པས། ཕར་བལྟས་རྒྱུད་ཀྱི་ཆོས་
བརྒྱ་ལས། །ཚུར་བལྟས་སེམས་ཀྱི་ཆོས་གཅིག་མཆོག །ཕར་ལ་ལྟ་

བའི་གཅེས་ཕྲུག་པོ། །དེ་རིང་རྩུར་ལ་བལྟ་བར་རིགས། ཞེས་སོ། །དེ་འདྲ་བའི་སྒྲ་བསམ་བརྗོད་དུ་མེད་པའི་རིག་པ་ཟང་ཐལ་སལ་ལེ་སེང་ངེ་རྗེན་ནེ་བ་འདི་ནི་རང་བྱུང་ཡེ་ཤེས་ཆེན་པོ་ཡིན་ལ། དེའི་ངང་ལས་ཚོགས་དྲུག་གི་ཡུལ་སྣང་གང་ཤར་ཐམས་ཅད་རང་བྱུང་ཡེ་ཤེས་འདིའི་རྩལ་རོལ་བ་དང་། རྒྱན་དུ་ཤེས་དགོས་པ་ནི། ལོ་ཆེན་བཻ་རོ་ཙ་ནའི་ཞལ་ནས། བརྗོད་མེད་རིག་པ་ཟང་ཐལ་ལེ། །བསམ་འདས་སེམས་ཀྱི་དྲི་མ་དག །རང་བྱུང་ཡེ་ཤེས་ངོ་བོ་ཉིད། །ཅི་སྣང་ཆོས་སྐུའི་རྒྱན་དུ་ཤར། །ཞེས་དང་། དཔལ་གྱི་ཡེ་ཤེས་ཀྱི་ཞལ་ནས། རང་བྱུང་ཡེ་ཤེས་བློ་ལས་འདས། །སེམས་ཉིད་ནམ་མཁའ་མཐའ་དབུས་མེད། །ཚོགས་བརྒྱད་སྣང་བ་ངོས་བཟུང་བྲལ། །རང་བྱུང་དགོངས་པ་འདི་ཀ་འོ། །ཞེས་རང་བྱུང་རིག་པའི་ཡེ་ཤེས་དེ་ནི་བློ་རྟོག་གཉིས་འཛིན་ཅན་གྱི་ཡུལ་ལས་འདས་པའི་སེམས་ཀྱི་གནས་ལུགས་དེ་ཁོ་ན་ཉིད་ནམ་མཁའ་ལྟ་བུའི་སྟེང་འོག་མཐའ་དབུས་ཕྱོགས་དང་ཕྱོགས་མཚམས་གང་ཡང་མ་གྲུབ་པའི་ཀ་ནས་དག་པའི་ཡེ་ཤེས་སྤྲོས་བྲལ་མཉམ་པ་ཉིད་དེ་ཡིན་པས། དེའི་ངང་དུ་ཚོགས་བརྒྱད་ཀྱི་སྣང་བ་གང་ཤར་ཀྱང་། རང་ཤར་རང་གྲོལ་ཆེན་པོའི་ངང་བསྐྱངས་ན་དེ་ལས་གཞན་ཅི་ཡང་མེད་དོ། །གཞན་ཡང་འཇིགས་མེད་བསྟན་ཉིས། འདིར་བསྒོམ་ཟེར་རྒྱུའི་ངོ་བོ་ངོས་བཟུང་དུ་མེད་ཀྱང་གསལ་སྟོང་བརྗོད་མེད་ཀྱི་ངོ་བོ་ཧ་གོ་བཞིན་དེའི་ངང་མ་ཤོར་བར་བསྐྱང་ན་རེད་ཡོད། །ཅེས་དང་། མི་ཕམ་རིན་པོ་ཆེས། རིག་ཐོག་ན་ཡོད་དུས་བལྟས་པ་འདྲ་བ། མཐོང་རྒྱུ་གང་ཡང་མེད་པ། མ་མཐོང་ཀྱང་གཏིང་ནས་གསལ་བ། ཡེངས་ཀྱང་ངོ་བོ་མི་འགྱུར་བ། མ་ཡེངས་ཀྱང་གཏད་སོ་དང་བྲལ་བ་ཞིག་དགོས་སོ། །ཞེས་གསུངས། དེ་ལྟར་ཐོས་བསམ་དང་གཏན་ཚིགས་ཀྱི་གོ་བ་ཙམ་མ་ཡིན་པར། ཉམས་མྱོང་གི་སྟེང་ནས་སེམས་གཞི་མེད་རྩ་བ་དང་བྲལ་བའི་སྐྱེ་བ་མེད་ཀྱང་དྭངས་གསལ་འགག་པ་མེད་པའི་སྟོང་སེང་ངེ་། དྭངས་སལ་ལེ་ཡངས་

ཁྲོལ་ལེ་བའི་རིག་པ་གཅེར་བུ་རྗེན་པ་ལས་གཞན་ངོ་བོ་ངོས་རྒྱ་བཟུང་ཅི་ཡང་མེད་དེ་ཉམས་མགུར་ལས། གང་ཤར་ཁྲེགས་ཆོད་ཀྱི་ཤེས་རབ་རལ་གྲི། ཐད་ཀ་ཁོལ་བྱུང་གི་སེམས་ལ་བཏབ་པས། །དེ་ཡིན་འདི་མིན་གྱི་ངོས་བཟུང་བྲལ་ཙམ། །ངོ་བོ་བསྐྱུང་རྒྱ་དེ་ཨེ་ཡིན་སྙམ་མོ། །ཞེས་གསུངས་པ་ལྟར་རོ། །འདིར་ཚིག་གསུམ་གནད་དུ་རྡེག་པའི་དང་པོ་ངོ་རང་ཐོག་ཏུ་སྤྲོད་པ་ཡིན་ལ། དེའི་དོན་ནི་ལྟ་བའི་ངོ་མ་འཕྲོད་ན་སྒོམ་པས་དང་སྐྱོང་ཐབས་མེད་པས་ན། ཐོག་དང་པོ་ངོ་འཕྲོད་པ་གལ་ཆེ། དེ་ཡང་རིག་པ་འདི་ཉིད། གཞན་ནས་བཙལ་དུ་ཡོད་པ་མ་ཡིན། སྔར་མེད་རང་རྒྱུད་ལ་སྐྱེས་པའང་མ་ཡིན། རང་ལ་ཡེ་ནས་འབྲལ་མེད་དུ་ཡོད་པའི་ལྷན་གཅིག་སྐྱེས་པའི་ཡེ་ཤེས་དེ་ཉིད་ངོ༷་རང་ཐོག༷་ཏུ་སྤྲོད༷་པ༷་སྟེ༷་གནད༷་དང༷་པོ༷འོ༷། ||

༄ གཉིས་པ་ཐག་གཅིག་ཐོག་ཏུ་བཅད་པ་ནི། དེ་ནས་འགྲོ་འམ་གནས་ཀྱང་རུང་། །ཁྲོ་འམ་ཆགས་སམ་སྐྱིད་དམ་སྡུག །དུས་དང་གནས་སྐབས་ཐམས་ཅད་དུ། །ངོ་ཤེས་ཆོས་སྐུ་ངོས་བཟུང་ལ། །སྔར་འདྲིས་འོད་གསལ་མ་བུ་སྤྲད། །བརྗོད་མེད་རིག་ཆའི་ངང་ལ་བཞག ། གནས་བདེ་གསལ་འགྲོ་ཡང་ཡང་བཤིག །ཐབས་ཤེས་ཡི་གེ་ཕྚ་བུར་འབེབས། །མཉམ་བཞག་རྗེས་ཐོབ་ཐ་དད་མེད། །ཐུན་དང་ཐུན་མཚམས་དབྱེ་བ་མེད། །དབྱེར་མེད་ངང་དུ་རྒྱུན་དུ་གནས། །འོན་ཀྱང་བརྟན་པ་མ་ཐོབ་བར། །འདུ་འཛི་སྤངས་ནས་སྒོམ་པ་གཅེས། །མཉམ་བཞག་ཐུན་དུ་བཅད་ལ་བྱ། །དུས་དང་གནས་སྐབས་ཐམས་ཅད་དུ། ། ཆོས་སྐུ་གཅིག་པུའི་ཡོ་ལངས་བསྐྱང་། །དེ་ལས་གཞན་མེད་ཁོ་ཐག་བཅད། །ཐག་གཅིག་ཐོག་ཏུ་བཅད་པ་སྟེ་གནད་གཉིས་པའོ། །དེ༷་ལྟར་གནད་དང་པོ་སོང་ཟིན་ནས༷། ད་ནི་སྒོམ་པས་ཉམས་སུ་ལེན་སྐབས་གནས་ན་ཆོས་སྐུའི་རང་ངོ་། འགྲོ་ན་ཡེ་ཤེས་ཀྱི་རང་རྩལ་ཡིན་པར་ངོས་ཟིན་ན། གནས་ན་རིག་པའི་ངང་། འགྲོ་ནའང་རིག་པའི་ངང་ཡིན་པས་ན། འགྲོ༷

འམ་གནས་ཀྱང་རུང་སྟེ་གང་ལྟར་ཡང་རིག་སྟོང་སྐྱེ་བ་མེད་པའི་ངང་དུ་གློད་
ཤེས་ན། སྒོམ་དང་མི་སྒོམ་ཇི་ལྟར་གནས་ཀྱང་ཡེངས་པ་མེད་དེ། ཀུན་
བྱེད་ལས། དྲན་བསམ་ཡིད་ལ་འགྱུ་བ་མ་ལུས་ཀུན། །སྐྱེ་བ་མེད་པའི་
ངང་ལས་མི་ཡེངས་བར། །གང་ལྟར་བསམས་ཀྱང་སྒོམ་པ་ཡིན་ཤེས་
ན། །མ་བསྒོམས་གང་ལྟར་བཞག་ཀྱང་ཡེངས་པ་མེད། །ཅེས་གསུངས་
པའི་དགོངས་དོན་རྟོགས་ན་གནས་པ་སྒྲུབ་མི་དགོས། འགྲོ་བ་དགག་མི་
དགོས་པར་ངང་བཞག་ཆུ་བོའི་རྒྱུན་ནམ་སྒོམ་མེད་ཆུ་བོའི་རྒྱུན་གྱི་ཉིང་ངེ་འཛིན་
ལས་ནམ་ཡང་མི་འདའ་བ་ཡིན་ཏེ། ཞབས་དཀར་བས། ཕར་ལ་བློ་
ཡིས་བཅོས་པ་མ་ཡིན་པར། །ཚུར་ལ་རྩ་བརྒྱུད་བླ་མའི་བྱིན་རླབས་
ལས། །ཤར་བ་མཁའ་ལྟར་དག་པའི་ལྟ་བ་དེ། །རྒྱུན་ཆད་མེད་པར་ཆུ་
བོའི་གཞུང་བཞིན་དུ། །མ་ཡེངས་དྲན་པས་རྒྱུན་དུ་སྐྱོང་བ་ལ། །སྒོམ་
མེད་ཆུ་བོའི་རྒྱུན་གྱི་ཉིང་འཛིན་ཟེར། །ཞེས་གསུངས་པ་ལྟར་རོ། །དེ་
བཞིན་དུ་ངོས་ཟིན་ན་རིག་པ་རང་བཞག་བདེ་བ་ཆེན་པོ་མ་བསྒོམས་ལྷུན་གྱིས་
གྲུབ་པའི་བསམ་གཏན་ཟེར་བ་དེ་ད་ལྟའི་དུས་ན་ཆུ་བོའི་གཞུང་ཆེན་བཞིན་ཡོད་
པ་ནི། རིག་པ་མ་བཅོས་མཉམ་པར་བཞག་ན་ངང་ངམ་ཤུགས་ཀྱིས་གསལ་
ནུས་ཏེ། གནས་ལུགས་མཛོད་ལས། རང་བཞག་བདེ་བ་ཆེན་པོ་རྡོ་རྗེའི་
དབྱིངས། །མ་བསྒོམས་ལྷུན་གྱིས་གྲུབ་པའི་བསམ་གཏན་མཆོག །རྟག་
ཏུ་ཡོད་དེ་ཆུ་བོའི་གཞུང་ཆེན་འདྲ། །མ་བཅོས་མཉམ་པར་བཞག་ན་ངང་
གིས་གསལ། །ཞེས་གསུངས་པ་ལྟར་རོ། །དེ་ལྟར་གནས་ཚེ་ཡུལ་ཡིད་
དུ་མི་འོང་བ་ལ་བརྟེན་ནས་ཁོང་ཁྲོ་འམ་ཞེ་སྡང་གི་རྟོག་པ་སྐྱེས་ཀྱང་རུང་།
ཡུལ་ཡིད་དུ་འོང་བ་ལ་བརྟེན་ནས་འདོད་ཆགས་ཀྱི་རྟོག་པ་སྐྱེས་སམ།
ཡང་ན་སེམས་བདེ་ཞིང་སྐྱིད་པའི་སྣང་བ་ཤར་ཀྱང་རུང་། ཡང་ན་སེམས་
མི་བདེ་བ་སྡུག་བསྔལ་བའི་སྣང་བ་དང་། རྣམ་པར་རྟོག་པ་གང་ཤར་ཐམས་
ཅད་རིག་པ་ཆོས་ཉིད་ཀྱི་ཡོ་ལངས་དང་། རིག་པ་ཆོས་ཉིད་ཀྱི་རྩལ་རོལ་བ་

རུ་ཤེས་དགོས། ཤེས་ནས་དུག་ལྔ་མ་སྤངས་ཡེ་ཤེས་ལྔ་རུ་གནས་གྱུར་བའི་མན་ངག་གལ་ཆེ། དེས་ན་དུས་དང་གནས་སྐབས་ཐམས་ཅད་དུ་འཁྲུལ་འཁྲུམས་ཐ་མལ་གྱི་རྟོག་པའི་དབང་དུ་མ་ཤོར་བར། སྔར་བླ་མས་ངོ་སྤྲོད་པའི་རིག་སྟོང་སྤྲོས་བྲལ་ཐིག་ལེ་ཉག་གཅིག་ཏུ་ངོ་ཤེས། གང་ཤར་ཐམས་ཅད་ཆོས་སྐུའི་རིག་པ་འབའ་ཞིག་མ་གཏོགས་གཞན་དུ་མེད་པར་ངོས་ཟུངས་ལ། ཚོགས་དྲུག་གི་ཡུལ་སྣང་དང་འཁྲུལ་རྟོག་གི་སྣང་བ་ཐམས་ཅད་གང་ཤར་ཡང་སྤང་བླང་གང་ཡང་མེད་པར་རང་བབས་སུ་བཞག་དགོས། དུག་ལྔའི་རྟོག་པ་གང་ཤར་ཀྱང་དེ་དང་དེའི་སྐབས་དུ་ངོ་བོ་ལ་མི་བལྟ། རྗེས་སུ་ཡང་མི་འབྲང་། གཉེན་པོ་བརྟེན་པ་ལྟ་བུའི་རྟང་རྟེག་ཀྱང་མི་བྱེད་པར་རྒྱན་པོས་བྱ་རྒྱང་གི་སྤྱོད་པ་ལ་བལྟ་བ་བཞིན་རེ་དོགས་མི་བྱེད་པར་རང་གར་བསྐྱུར་ཏེ་རིག་པ་ཆོས་སྐུའི་ངང་ལས་མི་གཡོ་བར་བཞག་གོ །ཉོན་མོངས་པའི་རྟོག་པ་སོགས་རྣམ་རྟོག་གང་ཤར་ཀྱང་དེ་དག་གི་ངོ་བོ་ཡེ་ནས་དྲི་མ་ཐམས་ཅད་དང་བྲལ་བའི་ཡེ་སྟོང་ནམ་མཁའ་ལྟ་བུ་དེ་ཆོས་སྐུ་གཞིར་གནས་ཀྱི་འོད་གསལ་ལམ། གཞིའི་རིག་པ་མ་ལྟ་བུའི་ཐ་སྙད་སྦྱར་བ་དང་། ད་ལྟ་བླ་མའི་ངོ་སྤྲོད་པའི་འོད་གསལ་བའི་རིག་པ་དེ། ལམ་གྱི་འོད་གསལ་བུའི་ཐ་སྙད་སྦྱར་ཏེ། སྙིང་གི་དམར་ཁྲིད་ལས། ཆོས་ཐམས་ཅད་ཀྱི་རང་བཞིན་མེད་པ་དེ་ཆོས་ཉིད་མ། རང་བཞིན་མེད་པར་ཤེས་པ་དེ་ཆོས་ཉིད་བུ་གསུངས། སྔར་འདྲིས་པའི་གཞི་ལམ་གྱི་འོད་གསལ་ཟུང་འཇུག་དབྱེར་མི་ཕྱེད་པའི་རང་ངོ་ལ་བལྟ་བ་ནི། འོད་གསལ་མ་བུ་སྤྲད་པ་ཞེས་བྱའོ། །དཔལ་སྤྲུལ་རིན་པོ་ཆེས། །སྔར་འདྲིས་འོད་གསལ་མ་བུ་སྤྲད། །ཞེས་པའི་ཐད། ཚོགས་དྲུག་གི་ཡུལ་སྣང་སོགས་ཀྱི་སྟེང་དུ་རྣམ་རྟོག་གང་ཤར་ཀྱང་རྣམ་རྟོག་ཤར་ཚད་ཐམས་ཅད་ཀྱི་གཤིས་སམ་ངོ་བོ་ནི་སྤྲོས་བྲལ་མཉམ་ཉིད་ཀྱི་ཡེ་ཤེས་ཆེན་པོ་ཆོས་སྐུ་གཞིའི་འོད་གསལ་ལམ། ཆོས་སྐུ་གཞིར་གནས་ཀྱི་ཡེ་ཤེས་ཡིན་པས་ན། འདི་ལ་གཞིའི་འོད་གསལ་མའི་ཐ་སྙད་

བཞག་པ་དང་། ད་ལྟ་བླ་མས་ངོ་སྤྲོད་པའི་རང་རིག་ཟང་ཐལ་གྱི་རིག་ཆ་
རྗེན་པར་ཤར་བ་འདི་འོད་གསལ་བུའི་ཐ་སྙད་བཞག་སྟེ། ལམ་གྱི་འོད་
གསལ་དེ་གཞིའི་འོད་གསལ་མཐའ་དབུས་དང་བྲལ་བའི་དབྱིངས་སུ་དབྱེར་
མེད་དུ་འདྲེས་པ་ལ་འོད་གསལ་མ་བུ་འཕྲོད་པ་ཞེས་ཟེར། དེ་བཞིན་དུ་བདུད་
འཇོམས་པའི་ཞལ་རྒྱུན་སྣང་སྤྲུང་སྐབས་ལྟར། ལམ་གྱི་རིག་པ་ནི་བུམ་ནང་
གི་ནམ་མཁའ་དང་། ཕོར་བའི་ནང་གི་ཆུ་ཐིགས་ལྟར་རྒྱ་ཆུང་ལ།
གཞིའི་རིག་པ་མཐའ་གྲོལ་ཆེན་མོ་ཁྱབ་གདལ་ནམ་མཁའི་ཁོར་ཡུག་གཞི་མེད་
རྩ་བྲལ་ཆེན་མོ། ཡུལ་མེད་ཟང་ཐལ་གྱི་རོལ་བ། འཁོར་འདས་ཀུན་
ཁྱབ་ཀྱི་བདག་ཉིད་ཅན་ནོ། །དེས་ན་ལམ་གྱི་རིག་པ་རྒྱ་ཆུང་ཞིང་གུ་དོག་པ་
བུམ་ནང་གི་ནམ་མཁའ་ལྟ་བུ་དེ། བུམ་པ་ཐོ་བས་བཅག་ཚེ་བུམ་ནང་གི་
ནམ་མཁའ་ཕྱིའི་ནམ་མཁའ་དང་འདྲེས་དེ་ནམ་མཁའ་གཉིས་དབྱེར་མེད་དུ་
གྱུར་བ་བཞིན། ལམ་གྱི་རིག་ལ་དེ་གཞི་ཐོག་ཏུ་ཕེབས་པའམ་གཞི་རིག་དང་
འདྲེས་ཚེ་གཞིའི་རིག་པ་མཐའ་གྲོལ་ཆེན་པོ་མངོན་དུ་གྱུར་པ་ཡིན་ཞིང་། དེ་
འདྲའི་རྣལ་འབྱོར་དེ་ལ་ཁྱབ་གདལ་ནམ་མཁའི་རྣལ་འབྱོར་པ་ཟེར། ཞེས་
གསུངས། འདིས་ཀྱང་འོད་གསལ་མ་བུ་འདྲེས་ཚུལ་གསལ་བར་བསྟན།
དེ་བཞིན་དུ་དང་པོ་ངོ་འཕྲོད་ཀྱི་རིག་པ་སྐྱ་རེངས་དང་པོ་ལྟ་བུ། བར་དུ་
གདེང་ཐོབ་ཀྱི་རིག་པ་མཉམ་རྗེས་དང་བྲལ་བ་ནམ་ལངས་པ་ལྟ་བུ། མཐར་
གྲོལ་ཐོབ་ཀྱི་རིག་པ་ཉི་མ་ཤར་བ་ལྟ་བུ་ཞེས། ཞལ་རྒྱུན་འདིས་ཀྱང་འོད་
གསལ་མ་བུ་རིམ་བཞིན་འདྲེས་ཚུལ་བསྟན། སྤྱིར་གང་ཟག་རིམ་གྱིས་པ་
རྣམས་ལ་ངོ་ཤེས་རྩལ་རྫོགས་བརྟན་པ་ཐོབ་པ་རྣམས་རིམ་བཞིན་འོང་དགོས་པ་
ཡོངས་གྲགས་ལྟར་ཡིན་ཏེ། རྡོ་གྲུབ་འཇིགས་མེད་བསྟན་ཉིས། བསྒོམ་
བྱ་ངོ་བོའི་རིག་པ་དང་། སྒོམ་བྱེད་ཐུགས་རྗེའི་རིག་པ་གཉིས་ཡོད་པས།
སྒོམ་བྱེད་ཐུགས་རྗེའི་རིག་པའམ་རྩལ་གྱི་རིག་པ་འདི་ཉིད་གོམས་པ་ལ་བརྟེན་
ནས། བསྒོམ་བྱ་ངོ་བོའི་རིག་ཐོག་ཏུ་སྐྱེལ་དགོས་པར་གསུངས་པས་ན།

བསྒྲིགས་བཅད་བརྡར་བའི་གསེར་བཞིན་དུ་ཇེ་གསལ་དུ་འོང་བ་འདིས་ཀྱང་
ཤེས། དབང་རྣོན་ཐོས་གྲོལ་ཅིག་ཆར་བ་ཡིན་ན་བླ་མས་ངོ་སྤྲོད་བཏབ་པ་
ཙམ་གྱིས་འོད་གསལ་མ་བུ་དབྱེར་མེད་དུ་འདྲེས་ནས་ཡེངས་ཡུལ་ཆོས་ཉིད་དུ་
ཤར། ལྷ་སྒོམ་ཅིག་ཆོད་དུ་འགྲོ། སྣང་སེམས་དབྱེར་མེད་དུ་འདྲེས་འགྲོ་
བ་སྲིད་ཀྱང་དེ་འདྲ་ནི་རེ་རེ་ཙམ་མོ། །འདི་དག་དགོན་པོ་བསམ་འགྲུབ་ཚང་
གི་ཞལ་རྒྱུན་ནོ། །སྤྱིར་སེམས་ཀྱི་རང་བཞིན་ཡེ་ནས་འོད་གསལ་དུ་
བཞུགས་པ་དེ་གཞི་ཡི་འོད་གསལ་དང་། དེ་ཉིད་བླ་མའི་མན་ངག་ལ་བརྟེན་
ནས་སད་པར་བྱས་པ་དེ་ལམ་གྱི་འོད་གསལ་ཟེར། གཟོད་སྒྲིབ་པ་དག་ནས་
འབྲས་བུ་མངོན་དུ་གྱུར་བ་དེ་འབྲས་བུའི་འོད་གསལ་ཡིན་ནོ། །སྨྲ་བསམ་
བརྗོད་དུ་མེད་པའི་རིག་པ་སྟོང་གསལ་འགགས་མེད་ཀྱི་རང་ཞལ་མངོན་དུ་
བྱས་ཏེ་རིག་ཆ་རྗེན་པ་དེའི་ངང་ལ་རང་བབས་སུ་བཞག་པ་ནི་གནད་ཀྱི་ཡང་
གཅེས་དམ་པ་ཡིན་ནོ། །ལས་དང་པོ་བའི་སྐབས་ན་ལྷ་བ་ངོ་འཕྲོད་ནས་
སྒོམ་པའི་རྒྱུན་བསྐྱངས་ཆེ་གནས་བདེ་གསལ་སྤྲོའི་ཉམས་ལ་ཞེན་ན། རིག་
པའི་རང་ཞལ་སྒྲིབ་པས་ན་ཉམས་དེ་གསུམ་གྱི་ཤུན་པ་དང་བྲལ་ཏེ་རིག་པའི་
གཤིས་ལུགས་མངོན་དུ་གྱུར་ནས་རྣམ་པར་མི་རྟོག་པའི་ཡེ་ཤེས་སྐྱེ་དགོས།
དེས་ན་གནས་བདེ་གསལ་སྤྲོའི་ཉམས་ལ་ཞེན་ན་སྒོམ་པ་འཁྲུལ་བའི་ལམ་དུ་
གོལ་བས་ན། ཉམས་དེ་གསུམ་ཡང་ཡང་བཤིག་ནས་རིག་པའི་རང་གཤིས་
བསྐྱང་དགོས། རིག་པའི་རང་གཤིས་མ་ཤོར་ན། བདེ་གསལ་མི་རྟོག་
པའི་ཉམས་གང་ཤར་ཀྱང་དེ་དང་དེས་དྲངས་བའི་ཏིང་འཛིན་རང་རྒྱུད་ལ་
འཁྲུངས་བ་དང་། རིག་པ་བོགས་སྐྱེད་ཐོན་པའི་གྲོགས་དང་། རིག་པ་
སྐུ་གསུམ་གྱི་སྒྲུབ་གཞི་ཡིན་ཏེ། དེ་དག་གིས་དྲངས་པའི་ངོ་བོ་མི་རྟོག་པའི་
སྟོང་ཉམས་ནམ་མཁའི་དཀྱིལ་ལྟ་བུའི་རྒྱ་ཆེ་བ། རང་བཞིན་གསལ་བའི་
ཉམས་ཀུན་གསལ་ཉི་ཟླའི་དཀྱིལ་འཁོར་ལྟར་བག་ཡངས་པ། ཐུགས་རྗེ་
གྲོལ་ཉམས་རང་ཤར་རང་གྲོལ་བྱ་ལམ་རྗེས་མེད་དུ་གྱུར་ཏེ། རིག་ངོ་རྗེན་

ལ་བྱུང་བའི་ཡེ་ཤེས་ཁོང་ནས་གསལ་འོང་ངོ་། །དེ་ལྟར་མིན་པར་བདེ་གསལ་མི་རྟོག་པའི་ཉམས་མྱོང་ཞེན་ཅན་སྐྱེས་ན་ཡ༷ང་ཡ༷ང་བཤི༷ག་དགོས་ཏེ། ཇི་སྐད་དུ། རྣལ་འབྱོར་སྒོམ་པ་བཤིག་གྱིན་བཟང་། །ཕུ་ཆུ་དྲག་པོ་བརྡབ་གྱིན་བཟང་། །ཞེས་པ་ལྟར་རོ། །དེའང་ཇི་ལྟར་བཤིག་ཅེ་ན། གནས་བདེ་གསལ་སྤྲོའི་ཉམས་ཤར་ཚེ། དེ་ལ་བརྟེན་ནས་དགའ་སྤྲོ་སྐྱིད་སྣང་ལ་ཞེན་པ་སྐྱེ་སྐབས་ཕཊ་སྒྲ་དྲག་པོས་གཏོར་དགོས། རྒྱལ་བ་ཐམས་ཅད་ཀྱི་བྱིན་གྱིས་རླབས་པའི་སྤྱོད་བྱེད་ཐབ༷ས་ཀྱི་ཡི་གེ་ཕ་དང་། གཅོད་བྱེད་ཤེ༷ས་རབ་ཀྱི་ཡི༷་གེ༷་ཊ་གཉིས་ཟུང་དུ་འཇུག་པའི་ཡི་གེ་ཕཊ་སྒྲ་དྲག་པོ་ཐོག་ལྟུང་བ་ལྟ་བུ་གློ༷་བུ༷ར་དུ་འབེབ༷ས་པར་བྱས་པས་ཉམས་ཞེན་གྱི་ཤུན་པ་ཐམས་ཅད་ཐལ་གྱིས་གཏོར་ཏེ། རང་གནས་ཀྱི་ཡེ་ཤེས་གསལ་སྟོང་བརྗོད་མེད་ཀྱི་རིག་ཆ་རྗེན་པ་མངོན་དུ་གྱུར་བའི་ངང་སྐྱོང་དགོས་སོ། །མཉམ་བཞག་རྗེས་ཐོབ་ཐ་དད་མེད་ཅེས་པའང་སྤྱིར་ཆོས་སྐུ་གཞིར་གནས་ཀྱི་ཡེ་ཤེས་ཁོ་རང་གི་ངོ་བོའི་བཞུགས་ཚུལ་ནི། ཆོས་ཉིད་སྟོང་ཆའི་དབྱིངས་དང་། དེའི་གདངས་འགགས་པ་མེད་པའི་རིག་ཆ་གཉིས་ཟུང་དུ་འཇུག་པའི་སྤྲོས་བྲལ་མཉམ་ཉིད་ཆེན་པོའི་ངོ་བོ་ལ་མཉམ་བཞག་དང་རྗེས་ཐོབ་ཅེས་སོ་སོར་འབྱེད་དུ་མེད་པ་སློས་ཅི་དགོས། དེ་བཞིན་དུ་དབང་རྣོན་ཅིག་ཆར་བ་ཞིག་ཡིན་ན་མཉམ་རྗེས་དབྱེར་མེད་དུ་འདྲེས་ཏེ་གང་ཤར་རིག་ཆ་རྗེན་པའི་རྣམ་ལྡན་དུ་སྐྱེ་བས་ན་དེ་ལ་མཉམ་བཞག་རྗེས་ཐོབ་སོ་སོར་དབྱེ་བ་མེད། འོན་ཀྱང་རང་ཅག་ལྟ་བུའི་ལམ་རིམ་གྱིས་པ་དག་གིས་བླ་མའི་མན་ངག་དང་རང་གི་ཉམས་མྱོང་གི་གནད་ལ་བརྟེན་ནས་བསྒོམ་པའི་སྐབས་ན་བརྗོད་མེད་ཀྱི་རིག་པ་ཟང་ཐལ་ལེ་བའི་ངང་དུ་དུས་དང་རྣམ་པ་ཀུན་ཏུ་མི་ཡེངས་པར་བསྒོམས་ཏེ་མཉ༷མ་བཞ༷ག་དང་རྗེ༷ས་ཐོ༷བ་གཉིས་ཀྱི་དབྱེ་བ་ཐ་ད༷ད་མེ༷ད་པར་སྒོམ་དགོས་ཞེས་བསྟན་པའོ། །དེ༷འང་ཐུན་གྱི་ངོ༷་བོ་ལ་རི༷ག་པ་མངོ༷ན་དུ་གྱུར་ཏེ་སྒོམ་པའི་རང་གཤིས་བསྐྱང་རྒྱུ་དང་། ཐུན་མཚམས་འགྲོ་འདུག་ཟ་ཉལ་སྤྱོད་ལམ་རྣམ་བཞིའི་སྐབས་

ཡེངས་པའི་དབང་དུ་ཤོར་ནས་རིག་པ་བོར་འགྲོ་བ་ལྟ་བུ་མ་ཡིན་པར། ཐུན་དང་ཐུན་མཚམས་དབྱེ་བ་མེད་པར་རིག་ཆ་འབའ་ཞིག་གི་ངང་ལས་ནམ་ཡང་མི་གཡོ་བ་ཞིག་དགོས་སོ། །དེ་བཞིན་དུ། བདུད་འཇོམས་པས། བསམ་མེད། སྒོམ་མེད། སྐྱོང་མེད། ཡེངས་མེད། འཆོ་མེད། ཅེས་གསུངས་པ་ལྟར་དང་། ཇི་སྐད་དུ། བསྒོམས་མ་སྐྱོང་དང་འབྲལ་མ་སྐྱོང་། །མི་སྒོམ་དོན་དང་མི་འབྲལ་བ། །ཞེས་པ་ལྟར་བསྒོམ་མེད་ཆུ་བོའི་རྒྱུན་གྱི་ཧྲིང་ངེ་འཛིན་རང་རྒྱུད་ལ་སྐྱེས་ན་རྩོལ་བཅས་ཀྱི་སྒོམ་པ་སྤྱུ་ཙམ་མེད་པས་བསྒོམ་མ་སྐྱོང་བ་དང་ངོ་བོའི་ངང་ལས་སྐད་ཅིག་ཀྱང་ཡེངས་པ་མེད་པས་འབྲལ་མ་སྐྱོང་བ་དང་། བསྒོམ་དུ་མེད་པའི་གནས་ལུགས་ཟབ་མོའི་དོན་ལས་ནམ་ཡང་མི་འདའ་བས་ན་མི་སྒོམ་དོན་དང་མི་འབྲལ་བ་ཞེས་སོ། །དེ་འདྲའི་གདེང་རླེད་མེད་པའི་རང་ལྟ་བུའི་ལམ་རིམ་གྱིས་པ་དག་གིས་ནམ་ཡང་དྲན་ཤེས་བརྟེན་ཏེ། དུས་དང་རྣམ་པ་ཀུན་ཏུ་བསྒོམས་མི་བསྒོམ་ཀྱི་དབྱེ་བ་མེད་པར་དབྱེར་མེད་ཀྱི་རིག་སྟོང་ཆོས་སྐུའི་རང་ཞལ་རྗེན་བྱུང་དང་ལ་རྒྱུན་དུ་གནས་དགོས་སོ། །དེ་བཞིན་དུ་དབང་པོ་ཆེས་རྣོན་པོ་ཅན་རང་བཞིན་རྫོགས་པ་ཆེན་པོའི་རང་ལམ་གྱི་སྦྲ་ཧེ་བཞིན་པའི་སྣོད་རུང་། ཐོས་གྲོལ་ཅིག་ཆར་དུ་འགྲོ་བའི་རིགས་ཅན། ཇི་སྐད་དུ། རྟོགས་གྲོལ་དུས་མཉམ་ཨིནྡྲ་བྷུ་ཏི་བཞིན་ཞེས་པ་ལྟར། ངོ་འཕྲོད་མ་ཐག་ཏུ་ཡེངས་ཡུལ་ཆོས་ཉིད་དུ་ཤར། ལྟ་སྒོམ་ཅིག་ཆོད་དུ་འགྲོ། སྣང་སེམས་གཞི་ཐོག་ཏུ་གྲོལ་བའི་གང་ཟག་ཡིན་ན་བསྒོམ་བྱ་སྒོམ་བྱེད་མེད་པས་ན། དེ་འདྲས་བསྒོམ་མི་དགོས་མོད། འོན་ཀྱང་དེ་ལས་གཞན་དུ་སྐལ་དམན་རིམ་གྱིས་པའི་གང་ཟག་རྣམ་རྟོག་འཁྲུལ་བའི་གཞན་དབང་དུ་གྱུར་པ་རྣམས་ཀྱིས་རིག་ཐོག་ཏུ་བརྟན་པ་མ་ཐོབ་ཀྱི་བར་དུ་སྒོམ་དགོས་ཏེ། འཇིགས་མེད་གླིང་པས། རིག་ངོ་འཕྲོད་ཀྱང་དེ་ངང་མ་གོམས་ན། །རྣམ་རྟོག་དགྲས་ཁྱེར་གཡུལ་ངོའི་བུ་ཆུང་བཞིན། །ཞེས་དང་། བསྒོམ་པ་མི་གཙོ་གོམས་པ་གཙོ། །

གོམས་པ་གླིང་དུ་གྱུར་ན་བསྒོམ་པའི་མཆོག །ཅེས་དང་། མ་ཐོས་པས་ཅི་ཤེས། མ་ཤེས་པས་ཅི་བསྒོམ། མ་བསྒོམས་པས་ཅི་གྲོལ། །ཅེས་སོ། །བརྟན་པ་ཐོབ་པའི་ཚད་རྨི་ལམ་གྱིས་འཛིན། རྟགས་སྤྱོད་པས་བསྲུམ་ཟེར་བ་ལྟར་ཡིན། སྒོམ་པའི་གནས་དེའང་འདུ་འཛི་རྣམ་གཡེང་གི་ཁྲོད་དུ་ཇི་ཙམ་སྒོམ་ཡུན་བསྲིངས་ཀྱང་རྟོགས་པ་ཁྱད་པར་ཅན་སྐྱེ་མི་ཐུབ་པའི་ཕྱིར། ཡང་དག་པའི་རྟོགས་པ་རང་རྒྱུད་ལ་སྐྱེ་དགོས་ན། འཇིག་རྟེན་སྤངས་བ། རྣམ་རྟོག་དོར་བ། དབེན་པ་བརྟེན་པ། ཚུལ་ཁྲིམས་སྲུང་བ། སྙིང་རྗེ་སྒོམ་པ། མོས་གུས་བསྐྱེད་པ། སྦྱིན་པ་སྤྱོད་པ་རྣམས་ནི་ཉམས་ལེན་གྱི་མཐུན་རྐྱེན་མེད་ཐབས་མེད་པ་ཡིན་པས་ན། དེ་ལྟར་བྱས་ནས་སྙིང་རུས་ཞེ་བཅད་དྲག་པོའི་སྒོ་ནས་སྒོམ་པ་ནི་ཤིན་ཏུ་གཅེས་པའི་ཆོས་ཡིན་ནོ། །སྒོམ་ཆེན་པ་རྣམས་ལ་རིག་ཐོག་གཅིག་ནས་ནམ་ཡང་གཡོ་འགྱུལ་མེད་པས་ན་དེ་འདྲ་དེ་ལ་མཉམ་བཞག་དང་རྗེས་ཐོབ་ཀྱི་ཁྱད་པར་མེད་དེ། རྗེས་ཐོབ་སྤྱོད་ལམ་གྱི་སྐབས་སུ་ལྟ་བའི་གདེང་མི་འཆོར། བསྒོམ་པའི་ངང་མི་འདའ་བར། ཉམས་མྱོང་གི་ཡེ་ཤེས་དེ་རྗེས་ཐོབ་སྤྱོད་ལམ་དང་བསྲེ་ནུས་པའི་ཁྱད་ཆོས་ཡོད་དོ། །དེ་འདྲ་མིན་པར་ལས་དང་པོ་བ་རང་ལྟ་བུ་དག་གིས་ཐུན་དུ་བཅད་ནས་སྒོམ་པའི་རང་དུས་ན། མཉམ་བཞག་དང་རྗེས་ཐོབ་ཀྱི་ཉམས་ལེན་གཉིས་ལ་ཁྱད་པར་མེད་པ་ལྟར་སྣང་ཡང་། ད་དུང་བརྟན་པ་མ་ཐོབ་པའི་རྐྱེན་གྱིས་རྗེས་ཐོབ་ཀྱི་སྐབས་སུ་མཉམ་བཞག་གི་ཡེ་ཤེས་དེ་རྗེས་ཐོབ་དང་བསྲེ་མི་ནུས་པ་ནི། མཉམ་བཞག་གིས་རང་ས་མ་ཟིན་པས་ལན་པ་ཡིན། དེ་འདྲ་དེས་མཉམ་བཞག་དང་རྗེས་ཐོབ་གཉིས་ཀྱི་ནང་ནས་མཉམ་བཞག་གཙོ་བོར་བྱས་ཏེ་ཉམས་ལེན་ཐུན་དུ་བཅད་ལ་ཐུན་བཞི་ལས་དྲུག་སོགས་ལ་བརྩོན་པའམ། ཡང་ན་ཇི་སྐད་དུ། ཡུན་ཐུང་གྲངས་མང་ཁང་སྟོང་ཐིགས་པ་བཞིན༔ ཞེས་པ་ལྟར། ཉིན་རེར་ཐུན་མང་པོར་སྦྱང་དགོས་པས་དེ་ལྟར་བསྒོམ་པར་བྱའོ། །དེ་ལྟར་མ་བྱས་ན་སྤྱོད་ལམ་རྒྱུན་གྱི་ལམ་

ཁྲེར་ལ་འབད་པར་བྱས་ཀྱང་སྤྱི་འབྱམས་གཞིས་ཤོར་གྱི་གོལ་ས་ལྷུང་ཉེས་ཆེ་
སྟེ། ལས་དང་པོ་བ་ཁ་ཅིག་ན་རེ། ང་རང་མཉམ་བཞག་ཐུན་དུ་བཅད་པ་
ལས་རྗེས་ཐོབ་སྤྱོད་ལམ་གྱི་སྐབས་སུ་མ་བརྗེད་པ་ཙམ་བྱས་ན་དེའི་བཟང་
འདུག་ཟེར་ཡང་། དེ་འདྲ་དེ་ལ་ཉེན་ཁ་ཆེ་ཞེས་མཁན་ཆེན་འཇིགས་མེད་
ཕུན་ཚོགས་ཀྱིས་གསུངས། དེ་ལྟར་དུས་དང་གནས་སྐབས་ཐམས་ཅད་དུ་
མཉམ་བཞག་གི་སྐབས་སུ་ཉམས་ལེན་ཐུན་དུ་བཅད་པ་དང་། རྗེས་ཐོབ་ཀྱི་
སྐབས་སུ་རྗེས་ཐོབ་སྤྱོད་ལམ་དང་བསྲེས་ནས་རྒྱུན་དུ་སྐྱོང་བ་གལ་ཆེ། དེ་
ལྟར་མ་བསྐྱངས་ན་མཉམ་བཞག་གི་ངོ་བོ་སྐྱོང་པའི་དུས་སུ་རང་གིས་རང་ལ་
བློ་གཏད་ཁེལ་ཚོག་པ་ལྟ་བུའི་ཉམས་ལེན་ཡོད་ཀྱང་། དེ་རྗེས་ཐོབ་སྤྱོད་
ལམ་དང་བསྲེས་ནས་རྒྱུན་དུ་སྐྱོང་མ་ཤེས་ན། རྣམ་རྟོག་གི་རྐྱེན་དབང་དུ་
ཤོར་ནས་སྒོ་གསུམ་ཐ་མལ་དུ་ལུས་པས་ཕན་པ་ཅི་ཡང་མེད་དོ། །དེས་ན་
རྗེས་ཐོབ་སྤྱོད་ལམ་རྣམ་བཞིའི་སྐབས་སུ་རྗེས་ཤེས་ཟང་ཐལ་སྐྱོང་བ་གལ་
ཆེའོ། །མཉམ་རྗེས་དབྱེར་མེད་ཀྱི་ཡེ་ཤེས་མ་སྐྱེས་ཀྱི་བར་དུ། མཉམ་
བཞག་སྐབས་དང་རྗེས་ཐོབ་སྐབས་གཉིས། ལས་དང་པོ་བའི་དུས་ན་
སྐབས་ཤན་སོ་སོར་ཕྱེས་ཏེ་མཉམ་བཞག་སྐབས་རིག་ངོ་སྐྱོང་། རྗེས་ཐོབ་
སྐབས་དེ་ཡང་ཡང་དྲན་པས་བསྐྱང་། སོ་སོའི་སྐྱེ་བོའི་སྐབས་ན་རྗེས་ཐོབ་
དྲན་པའི་སྟེང་དུ་འཇོག་པ་ལས། རྗེས་ཐོབ་ལ་རིག་ངོ་ཧི་བཞིན་མཐོང་བ་
དཀའ་འདུག །ཅེས་མཁན་ཆེན་འཇིགས་མེད་ཕུན་ཚོགས་རིན་པོ་ཆེས་
གསུངས་སོ། །དུས་དང་གནས་སྐབས་གང་ཡིན་ཡང་། རིག་སྟོང་ཆོས་
སྐུ་ཆེན་པོའི་ལྟ་བ་གཅིག་པུའི་ཡོ་ལངས་བསྐྱངས་ནས་འདུག་པ་ལས་གཞན་
པའི་བསྒོམ་བྱ་ཅི་ཡང་ལོགས་ན་མེད་པར་ཐག་ཆོད་དེ། འདོད་ཆགས་ཞེ་
སྡང་གཏི་མུག་ཅེས་སྤང་བྱ་ཞིག་དང་། བྱམས་སྙིང་རྗེ་བྱང་ཆུབ་ཀྱི་སེམས་
ཞེས་བླང་བྱ་ཞིག་ཀྱང་མེད་དོ། །མཉམ་བཞག་སྐབས་སྟོང་གསལ་འགགས་
པ་མེད་པའི་རང་རིག་རང་ཤེས་ཀྱི་རིག་ཀ་རྗེན་པའི་ངང་དུ་རང་བབས་སུ་

བཞག་ཆོ། དེའི་རྩལ་རོལ་བར་ཤར་བའི་བྱ་བྱེད་རྣམ་རྟོག་ཐམས་ཅད་དཔེར་ན་མི་རྒན་གྱིས་བྱིས་པའི་རྩེད་མོ་ལ་བལྟ་བ་བཞིན། དགག་སྒྲུབ་སྤང་བླང་། རེ་དོགས་རྩིས་གདབ་གང་ཡང་མེད་པར་རང་ཡན་ཅི་དགར་བསྒྱུར་བཏང་ཆོ། ནམ་ཞིག་ན་སྣང་སེམས་ཐམས་ཅད། ཁྲལ་ཁྲོལ། འལ་འོལ། ཆད་ཆོད། ཡད་ཡུད་དུ་འགྲོའོ། །མདོར་ན་རང་གི་སྒོ་གསུམ་མ་བཅོས་རང་བབས་སུ་བཞག་ཆོ། སེམས་ཀྱི་གནས་ལུགས་མ་བཅོས་སལ་ལེ། སང་ངེ་བའི་རིག་ཆ་རྗེན་པ་མངོན་དུ་གྱུར་བ་འདི་ནི། ལྷན་ཅིག་སྐྱེས་པའི་ཡེ་ཤེས་ཞེས་པ་དེའང་དེ་ཡིན། ཞི་ལྷག་དབྱེར་མེད་ཞེས་པའང་དེ་ཡིན། སྤྲོས་བྲལ་གཉུག་མའི་ཡེ་ཤེས་ཀྱང་དེ་ཡིན། གསང་སྔགས་རྡོ་རྗེ་ཐེག་པའི་རྒྱུད་སྡེ་ཐམས་ཅད་ཀྱི་མཐར་ཐུག་གི་སྙིང་པོའང་དེ་ཡིན། དབང་བཞི་པའི་དོན་གྱི་ཡེ་ཤེས་ཀྱང་དེ་ཡིན། རྒྱ་བོད་གསར་རྙིང་གི་གྲུབ་བརྙེས་ཐམས་ཅད་ཀྱི་དགོངས་བཅུད་ཀྱང་དེ་ཡིན། སྙན་རྒྱུད་སྐོར་གསུམ་གྱི་ཡང་སྙིང་ཡང་དེ་ཉིད་ཡིན་པས་ན། དེ༷་ལས༷་གཞ༷ན་པའི་རིག་པ་ཆོས་སྐུ་ཞེས་བྱ་བ་ཞིག་གཏན་ནས་མེད༷་པར་ཁྲོ༷་ཐབ༷་ནང་ནས་བཅུ༷ད་པར་བྱའོ། །ཞེས་སོ། །དེ་ལྟར་རང་རིག༷་སངས་རྒྱས་སམ་ཆོས་སྐུ་རང་གནས་ཀྱི་ཡེ་ཤེས་འཁྲུལ་མ་མྱོང་པའི་སངས་རྒྱས་དེ་རང་རྒྱུད་ལ་ཡོད་པར་བློ་ཐག་གཅིག་ཐོག༷་ཏུ་བཅུ༷ད་ནས་དེའི་ངང་བསྐྱངས་པ༷་སྦྱེ༷་གནད༷་ཀྱི་གསང་ཚིག༷་གཉི༷ས་པའོ༷།། ༄

གསུམ་པ་གདེང་གྲོལ་ཐོག་ཏུ་བཅའ་བའི་ཚུལ་བཤད་པ་ནི། དེ་ཆེ་ཆགས་སྡང་དགའ་སྡུག་དང་། །བློ་བུར་རྣམ་རྟོག་མ་ལུས་པ། །ངོ་ཤེས་ངང་ལ་རྗེས་མཐུད་མེད། །གྲོལ་ཆའི་ཆོས་སྐུ་ངོས་བཟུང་བས། །དཔེར་ན་ཆུ་ཡི་རི་མོ་བཞིན། །རང་ཤར་རང་གྲོལ་རྒྱུན་ཆད་མེད། །ཅི་ཤར་རིག་སྟོང་རྗེན་པའི་ཟས། །ཧི་འགྱུ་ཆོས་སྐུ་རྒྱལ་པོའི་རྩལ། །རྗེས་མེད་རང་དག་ཨ་ལ་ལ། །འཆར་ལུགས་སྤྱར་དང་འདྲ་བ་ལས། །གྲོལ་ལུགས་ཁྱད་པར་གནད་དུ་ཆེ། །འདི་མེད་སྒོམ་པ་འཁྲུལ་བའི་ལམ། །འདི་ལྡན་མ་

བསྒོམས་ཆོས་སྐུའི་ངང་། །གདེང་གྲོལ་ཐོག་ཏུ་བཅའ་བ་སྟེ་གནད་གསུམ་པའོ། །ཞེས་དེའང་འདིས་སྤྱོད་པ་དང་འབྲས་བུ་གཉིས་ཀ་བསྟན། གྲོལ་ཚུལ་གྱི་གནད་དང་མི་ལྡན་ན། སེམས་གནས་ངལ་གསོའི་སྒོམ་ཙམ་རེ་ཡོད་ཀྱང་། དེ་ནི་ཁམས་གོང་མ་ལས་མི་འཕགས་ཏེ། ཉམས་ལེན་ལ་ཤར་གྲོལ་གྱི་གདེང་མེད་ན། སེམས་ཞི་བར་གནས་པའི་སྟེང་དུ་ངལ་གསོ་བ་ཙམ་ནི། ཡུན་རིང་གི་མགྲོན་པོ་རེ་ཞིག་ངལ་གསོ་བ་དང་འདྲ། དཔེ་མུ་སྟེགས་ལྷག་སྤྱོད་པ་ལོ་བཅུ་གཉིས་ལ་བསམ་གཏན་དུ་གནས་པ་བཞིན་ནོ། །དང་པོ་ངོ་འཕྲོད། དེ་ནས་ཐག་ཆོད། དེ་རྗེས་གདངས་སུ་གྲོལ་བ་སོགས་ཀྱི་ལམ་ལ་ཞུགས་ནས་བསྒོམ་པ་དེའི་ཚེ་འདོད་པའི་ཡུལ་ཡིད་དུ་འོང་བ་ལ་དམིགས་ནས་ཆགས་པའི་སེམས་སྐྱེས་པའམ། མི་འདོད་པའི་ཡུལ་ཡིད་དུ་མི་འོང་བ་ལ་དམིགས་ནས་ཞེ་སྡང་དྲག་པོ་སྐྱེས་སམ། མཐུན་རྐྱེན་ཟས་གོས་གནས་མལ་ལོངས་སྤྱོད་སོགས་འབྱོར་བ་དང་ལྡན་པ་ལ་དགའ་བ་དང་། མི་མཐུན་པའི་རྐྱེན་ན་ཚ་རྒུད་པ་ཉེར་འཚེ་སོགས་ལ་བརྟེན་ནས་སྡུག་བསྔལ་བ་སོགས་གང་བྱུང་ཚེ། རིག་པ་རྩལ་དུ་ལྡོང་བ་ཡིན་པས་ན། རྩལ་དང་རོལ་པ་ཐམས་ཅད་གྲོལ་གཞིའི་ཡེ་ཤེས་ངོས་ཟིན་པར་བྱས་ན། དེའི་ཀློང་དུ་རང་ཤར་རང་གྲོལ་དུ་འགྲོའོ། །གྲོལ་ལུགས་ལ་སྤྱི་དང་བྱེ་བྲག་གཉིས་ལས། སྤྱི་ལའང་འབད་བཅས་དང་། འབད་མེད་གཉིས། འབད་བཅས་ནི། སྣང་བ་ཡུལ་གྱི་བློ་ཅན་གྱི་གང་ཟག་ཡིན་ན། རྣམ་རྟོག་གང་ཤར་ཀྱང་ངོས་བཟུང་ནས་རིག་པའི་ངང་དུ་བཞག་ཚེ། འཇུ་བ་གནས་དག་གི་དགོངས་པ་མངོན་དུ་གྱུར་བ་དེའོ། །འབད་མེད་ནི་རིག་པ་རང་སྣང་གི་བློ་ཅན་ཏེ། དེས་ན་རིག་ཆ་རྗེན་པ་མངོན་དུ་གྱུར་ཚེ། རྟོག་ཚོགས་གང་ཤར་ཐམས་ཅད་རྗེ་ཆེན་ལ་ཁ་བ་བབས་པ་ལྟར་རིག་པའི་ཀློང་དུ་རང་ཤར་རང་ཡལ་རྗེས་མཐུད་མེད་པར་གྲོལ་བ་དེའོ། །བྱེ་བྲག་ལ་གྲོལ་ཚུལ་ལྔ་ཡོད་དེ། ཡེ་གྲོལ་ཡིན་པས་བསྒྲུལ་གཞི་མེད། །རང་གྲོལ་ཡིན་པས་གཉེན་པོ་

མེད། །ཅེར་གྲོལ་ཡིན་པས་མཐོང་སར་གྲོལ། །ཤར་གྲོལ་ཡིན་པས་སྤུ་
གྲི་མེད། །གཅིག་གྲོལ་ཡིན་པས་ཟླ་བོ་མེད། །ཅེས་སོ། །རྫོགས་པ་
ཆེན་པོའི་ལུགས་ལ་དུག་ལྔའི་རྟོག་པ་གང་ཤར་ཀྱང་རང་གྲོལ་དང་ཤར་གྲོལ་དུ་
འགྲོ་བ་དང་། སྔགས་ལྟར་ན་དུག་ལྔ་ལམ་དུ་བྱེད་པའི་ཐབས་ལ་བརྟེན་ནས་
སྤྱིར་རྒྱ་གར་གྱི་གྲུབ་བརྙེས་གོང་མ་རྣམས་ལྟ་བུ། དཔེར་ན་གྲུབ་ཆེན་སྒེག་
མོ་རྡོ་རྗེ་ཆང་འཚོང་མས་འདོད་ཆགས་ལམ་དུ་བྱས་པ་དང་། དེ་བཞིན་དུ་
རིགས་ངན་ཡན་ལག་མེད་པས་ཞེ་སྡང་ལམ་དུ་བྱས་པ། གྲུབ་ཐོབ་ལྭ་བ་
པས་གཏི་མུག་ལམ་དུ་བྱས་པ། བྱིས་པའི་རྩེད་མོ་ཅན་གྱིས་རྩེད་མོ་ལམ་དུ་
བྱས་པ་ལྟར་ཡིན་ནོ། །དེས་ན་ཤར་གྲོལ་གྱི་གནད་དང་མི་ལྡན་ན་སེམས་
བྱུང་འོག་འཁྲུའི་རྣམ་རྟོག་ཐམས་ཅད་ཀྱིས་འཁོར་བའི་ལས་བསགས་པ་ཡིན་
པས་ཕྲ་རགས་ཀྱི་རྣམ་རྟོག་སོགས་གློ་བུར་རྣམ་རྟོག་མ་ལུས་པ་ཅི་སྐྱེས་ཐམས་
ཅད་ཤར་གྲོལ་རྗེས་མེད་དུ་སྐྱོང་པའི་གནད་འདི་གལ་ཆེ། གང་ཟག་གཅིག་
གི་རྒྱུད་ལ་མཚོན་ན། བཟང་རྟོག ངན་རྟོག །ལུང་མ་བསྟན་གསུམ་
ལས་མི་སྲིད། དེ་དག་ལས་ཀྱང་བཟང་རྟོག་གི་རྟོག་པ་འདི་ངོས་ཟིན་དཀའ་
སྟེ། དཔེར་ན་ཟས་གོས་གནས་མལ་ཡོ་བྱད་སོགས་ལ་བརྟེན་ནས་སྐྱིད་སྣང་
གི་རྟོག་པ་ཤར་ཆེ། གྲོལ་བ་ཕར་ཞོག །སྣང་བ་ལྟར་ཞེན། ཞེན་པ་
ལྟར་འཐས་ནས་ལས་བསག་པ་ཡིན། དེ་བཞིན་དུ་དད་པ་དང་སྙིང་རྗེ་ལྟ་བུ་
སྐྱེས་ཆེ། ཡུལ་དཀོན་མཆོག་གསུམ་དང་ཡུལ་ཅན་རང་གཉིས་ཀ་བདེན་
གྲུབ་ཏུ་འཛིན། དད་པ་དེའང་བདེན་གྲུབ་ཀྱི་རྣམ་པར་ཤར་བ་ལྟ་བུ་དང་།
སྙིང་རྗེའང་དེ་དང་མཚུངས། འཆི་བ་མི་རྟག་པའི་བློ་སྐྱེས་ན། སྐྱེ་འཆི་
མཚན་འཛིན་གྱི་རྟོག་པ་དབྱིངས་སུ་དེངས་དགོས། དེ་བཞིན་དུ་ངན་རྟོག
དང་ལུང་མ་བསྟན་གྱི་རྟོག་པའང་དེ་བཞིན་ནོ། །གྲོལ་གཞི་རིག་སྟོང་ཟུང་
འཇུག །གྲོལ་བྱ་བཟང་རྟོག་ངན་རྟོག་ལུང་མ་བསྟན་གྱི་རྟོག་པ་གསུམ།
གྲོལ་ཚུལ་རང་གྲོལ་ཅེར་གྲོལ་ཤར་གྲོལ་ཡེ་གྲོལ་གཅིག་གྲོལ་ལོ། །རིག་ཆ་

རྗེན་པ་མངོན་དུ་མ་གྱུར་ན། འོག་འགྱུའི་རྣམ་རྟོག་གི་དབང་དུ་ཤོར་ཤས་ཆེ། མཉམ་བཞག་ཕུབ་མ་ལྟ་བུ། འོག་འགྱུའི་རྟོག་པ་ཆུ་ལྟ་བུ་ཟེར། དེ་དག་གིས་ཀྱང་ལས་བསག་ནུས། དེ་བཞིན་དུ་ཀུན་གཞི་ལ་གོལ་ན་གཟུགས་མེད། ཀུན་གཞིའི་རྣམ་ཤེས་ཀྱིས་གཟུགས་ཁམས། རྣམ་རྟོག་རགས་པས་འདོད་ཁམས་སུ་འཕེན། རིག་པ་སྟོང་གསལ་འགག་མེད་ཀྱི་རིག་ཆ་རྗེན་པ་འདིས་ཁམས་གསུམ་གྱི་སྐྱེ་གནས་འགོག་ནུས་ཏེ་རིག་ཆ་མི་འཕྲོ་བས་འདོད་ཁམས་ཀྱི་སེམས་ལས་གྲོལ། གསལ་ཀྱང་མི་འཛིན་པས་གཟུགས་ཁམས་ཀྱི་སེམས་ལས་གྲོལ། མི་རྟོག་ཀྱང་རིག་གདངས་མ་འགགས་པས་གཟུགས་མེད་ཀྱི་སེམས་ལས་གྲོལ་བས་ན། འདི་ལ་ཁམས་གསུམ་ཡོངས་གྲོལ་གྱི་དགོངས་པ་ཟེར་རོ། །དེ་ལྟར་རྣམ་རྟོག་གང་ཤར་ཐམས་ཅད་འོག་འགྱུ་འཁྲུལ་འཁྲུམས་ཀྱི་དབང་དུ་མ་སོང་། བློས་བྱས་གཉེན་ནུ་མས་བལ་མཁལ་བ་ལྟ་བུ། ཕྲ་སྨོམ་འཧུར་བུའི་ཆ་འཧུར་དྲན་ལྟ་བུ་མ་ཡིན་པར་གཉུག་མའི་དྲན་པ་དང་མ་བྲལ་བར་བཞག་ན། དྲན་སྣང་ཡེ་ཤེས་ཀྱི་འཁོར་ལོ་ཞེས་པ་སྟེ། རྣམ་རྟོག་ཤར་ཙམ་ནས་དྲན་མཁན་ཆོས་ཉིད་དུ་གྲོལ་བ་ནི་སེམས་ངོ་སྐྱོང་ཚུལ་མཆོག་ཏུ་གྱུར་བ་ཡིན། དེས་ན་རྣམ་རྟོག་ཅི་ཤར་ཡང་རིག་པའི་རང་ངོ་ཤེས་པར་བྱས་ལ། ཤར་བའི་ཆ་དེ་བསྐྱུར་ལ་རིག་ཆ་རྗེན་པའི་ངང་ལ་བཞག་ན། གང་ཤར་ཐམས་ཅད་རང་ཤར་རང་གྲོལ་དུ་སོང་ནས། རྗེས་མཐུད་མེད་པར་ཆུ་ལ་རི་མོ་བྲིས་པ་ལྟར་འགྲོའོ། །དེས་ན་རྣམ་རྟོག་རང་གྲོལ་དུ་འགྲོ་རྒྱུ་གལ་ཆེ་མ་གཏོགས་རྣམ་རྟོག་རང་གྲོལ་དུ་མ་སོང་ན། རྣམ་རྟོག་ངོ་ཤེས་པ་ཙམ་གྱིས་འཁྲུལ་བའི་རྒྱུན་མི་ཆོད་པས་ན། རྣམ་རྟོག་ངོ་ཤེས་པ་དང་མཉམ་དུ་རིག་པའི་རང་ངོར་ཅེར་གྱིས་བཞག་པས་རྣམ་རྟོག་རང་ཡལ་དུ་སོང་བའམ་རང་སར་གྲོལ་བའི་སྐབས་ན་རང་གནས་ཀྱི་ཡེ་ཤེས་ཆོས་ཀྱི་སྐུ་སལ་ལེ་སང་ངེ་རྗེན་ནེ་མངོན་དུ་གྱུར་བ་དེ། སྤུར་འདྲེས་ཀྱི་ཡེ་ཤེས་ཡིན་པར་ངོས་བཟུང་ལ་དེའི་ངང་བསྐྱངས་པས། དཔེར་ན་ཆུ་ལ་རི་མོ་བྲིས་

མ་ཐག་ཏུ་རི་མོ་དེ་རང་ཡལ་རང་ཞིག་ཏུ་འགྲོ་བ་བཞིན་དུ། རྣམ་རྟོག་སྐྱེས་པ་དང་གྲོལ་བ་དུས་མཉམ་དུ་སོང་ནས་རིག་པ་ཆོས་སྐུ་ཆེན་པོའི་ངང་དུ་ནམ་ཡང་འདུ་འབྲལ་མེད་པ་ཞིག་འོང་ངོ་། །དེས་ན་ཇི་ལྟར་ཤར་ཀྱང་ཤར་དུ་ཆུག །ཤར་བ་མི་དགག །གནས་པ་མི་སྒྲུབ་པར། གང་ཤར་རིག་སྟོང་ཆོས་སྐུའི་ངང་དུ་བཞག་པའི་ཚེ་རང་ཤར་རང་གྲོལ་ལ་རྒྱུན་ཆད་མེད་ཅིང་རྟོག་པ་གང་ཤར་ཚད་ཐམས་ཅད་ཀྱི་ནང་ན་མི་གྲོལ་བའི་ཆོས་གཅིག་ཀྱང་མི་སྲིད་དོ། །ཅི་ཤར་རིག་སྟོང་རྗེན་པའི་ཟས་ཞེས་པ་ནི། དཔེར་ན་མི་ཞིག་ལ་མཆོན་ན། ཁ་ཟས་གང་ཟོས་ན་ལུས་ཀྱི་སྟོབས་ཤུགས་རྒྱས་བྱེད་དུ་འགྲོ་བ་བཞིན། དུག་ལྔའི་རྟོག་པ་ཤུགས་དྲག་པོ་བདོ་བ་ནི། དེ་དག་ཡེ་ཤེས་ལྔ་རུ་གནས་འགྱུར་ན། ཇི་སྐད་དུ། ཉོན་མོངས་རྟོག་པ་མང་ན་ཆོས་སྐུ་མང་། ཞེས་པ་བཞིན་རྟོག་པ་གང་ཤར་ཀྱང་ཆོས་སྐུའི་རྩལ་སྦྱོང་བའམ་ཆོས་སྐུའི་རིག་པ་མངོན་དུ་གྱུར་བྱེད་དང་རིག་པ་གསལ་ངར་དང་ལྡན་པའི་ཐབས་སམ་གྲོགས་སུ་གྱུར་བས་ན། རྟོག་པ་ཅི་ཤར་ཐམས་ཅད་རིག་སྟོང་རྗེན་པའི་སྟོབས་ཤུགས་རྒྱས་བྱེད་ཀྱི་ཁ་ཟས་ལྟ་བུའི་ཐ་སྙད་སྦྱར་ཏེ། རིག་སྟོང་རྗེན་པས་རྟོག་ཚོགས་ཟས་སུ་ཟ་བ་ཞེས་བརྗོད་དོ། །དེས་ན་རྣམ་རྟོག་གང་ཤར་ཐམས་ཅད་ཆོས་སྐུའི་རྩལ་དང་། རིག་པའི་ཟས་ཡིན་པར་ཤེས་དགོས། དེ་བཞིན་དུ་རྣམ་རྟོག་བཟང་ངན་བར་གསུམ་ཇི་འགྱུ་ནའང་རིག་པ་ཆོས་སྐུ་རྒྱལ་པོ་ཟང་ཐལ་སྲིབ་གཡོག་དང་བྲལ་བ་དེའི་རྩལ་དང་རོལ་བ་ལས་མ་འདས་པ་ཡིན་པ་དང་། རྩལ་རོལ་བ་ཐམས་ཅད་རང་ཤར་རང་གྲོལ་ཆེན་པོ་རིག་སྟོང་ཆོས་སྐུ་རང་གི་ཀློང་དུ་བྱ་ལམ་རྗེས་མེད་དུ་གྲོལ་བ་ཡིན་ནོ། །དེ་ལྟར་ཡང་ཡང་གོམས་འདྲིས་བྱས་ནས་བསྒོམས་པས་ནམ་ཞིག་གི་ཚེ། ང་དང་བདག་ཏུ་འཛིན་པའི་གང་ཟག་གི་བདག་འཛིན་དང་། ཕྱི་ནང་སྣོད་བཅུད་ཀྱི་ཆོས་ཐམས་ཅད་བདེན་པར་འཛིན་པའི་ཆོས་ཀྱི་བདག་འཛིན་གཉིས་རིག་སྟོང་སྤྲོས་བྲལ་མཉམ་པ་ཆེན་པོའི་ཀློང་དུ་རང་སར་གྲོལ། འབྲེལ་བའི་རྒྱུན་ཆད་དེ།

གང་ཤར་ཐམས་ཅད་རིག་པ་འབའ་ཞིག་ལས་གཞན་དུ་བཙལ་ཀྱང་མི་རྙེད་པ་ལྟ་བུ་དང་། དཔེར་ན་རྦ་རླབས་ཐམས་ཅད་རྒྱ་མཚོ་ལས་མི་གཞན་པ་བཞིན་དུ་གང་ཤར་ཐམས་ཅད་རིག་པའི་ཡེ་ཤེས་ཀྱི་ཀློང་དུ་རྗེས་མེད་རང་དག་རང་ཡལ་དུ་འགྲོ། དེའི་ཚེ་ན་གསེར་གླིང་ནས་ས་རྡོ་ཙལ་བ་མི་རྙེད་པ་བཞིན། གང་ཤར་ཐམས་ཅད་རིག་སྟོང་ཐིག་ལེ་ཉག་གཅིག་གི་ཀློང་དུ་གཉིས་མེད་དུ་འདྲེས་པ་ཆོས་སྐུ་ཁྱབ་གདལ་ཆེན་པོ་ཨ་ལ་ལ་ཞེས་ཤིན་ཏུ་ངོ་མཚར་བའི་ཚིག་གོ །དེ་བཞིན་དུ་རྗེས་ཐོབ་ཀྱི་སྐབས་སུ་རྣམ་པར་རྟོག་པ་འཆར་ལུགས་སྔར་དང་འདྲ་བར་རྟོག་པ་སྣ་ཚོགས་འཕྲོ་བ་ཡོད་ནའང་། ཇི་སྐད་དུ། འཆར་བ་དེ་ནི་ཐ་མལ་རྟོག་པ་འདྲ། གྲོལ་བ་དེ་ནི་རྣལ་འབྱོར་ཁྱད་ཆོས་ཡིན། །ཞེས་པ་ལྟར་རྣམ་རྟོག་སྒོམ་དུ་ཤར་བ་ཞེས། འདིའི་དུས་སུ་གང་ཤར་ཐམས་ཅད་སྒོམ་ཡིན། གང་ལྟར་ཤར་ཀྱང་གནས་པའི་གོ་ས་མི་བཀག །ཇི་ལྟར་གནས་ཀྱང་འཆར་ཆ་འགགས་པ་མེད་པ་དེ་འདྲ་ཞིག་ཡིན་ནོ། །དེས་ན་འཆར་རྒྱུ་མེད་པ་ཞིག་མིན་ཀྱང་། མི་གྲོལ་བའི་འཆར་ཆ་གཅིག་ཀྱང་མེད་པ་ཞིག་དགོས། ཐ་མལ་བས་རྣམ་རྟོག་ཤར་བ་ལྟར་ཞེན། ཞེན་པ་ལྟར་འཐས་ནས་ལས་བསགས་པ་ཡིན། རྣལ་འབྱོར་བའི་ངོར་གང་ལྟར་ཤར་ཀྱང་རིག་པ་ལ་ཕོར་རྒྱུ་མེད། རྣམ་རྟོག་ལ་ཐོབ་རྒྱུ་མེད་དེ། ཁང་སྟོང་ལ་ཀུན་མ་ཞུགས་པ་ལྟ་བུ་ཡིན། འདིའི་དུས་སུ་རྣམ་རྟོག་ལ་ནུས་ཤུགས་ཅུང་ཟད་མེད་པ། དཔེར་ན་དབྱིད་ཀ་ས་གཞི་ལ་དྲོད་ཕེབས་ཚེ། སེར་བུ་གཡུག་ཀྱང་གྲང་རེག་གི་གདུག་རྩུབ་ཞི་ནས་ངར་ཤུགས་མེད་པ་ལྟ་བུའོ། །དྲེས་མའི་ཐག་པ་མེར་ཚིག་པའི་དཔེ་ལྟར། ལས་བསག་ཏུ་མེད་པ་ཡིན་ནོ། །འཁྲུལ་སྣང་རང་ཞིག་ཏུ་འགྲོ་ཞིང་རིག་པས་ཕར་འཁྲུལ་སྣང་གནོམ་ནུས་ཞིང་། རིག་པ་ཚུར་གང་གིས་ཀྱང་གནོམ་མི་ནུས་པ། རྡོ་རྗེ་ཕ་ལམ་ལས་གྲུབ་པའི་རལ་གྲི་དང་། རྡོ་རྗེ་ལྟ་བུའོ། །དེའང་དང་པོ་རྣམ་རྟོག་ངོ་ཤེས་པས་གྲོལ་བ་སྔར་འདྲིས་ཀྱི་མི་དང་འཕྲད་པ་ལྟ་བུ། བར་དུ་རྣམ་རྟོག

རང་གིས་རང་གྲོལ་བ་སྤྲུལ་གྱི་མདུད་པ་ལྟ་བུ། ཐ་མ་རྣམ་རྟོག་ཕན་མེད་གནོད་མེད་དུ་གྲོལ་བ་ཁང་སྟོང་དུ་རྐུན་མ་ཞུགས་པ་ལྟ་བུ་སྟེ། གྲོལ་ལུགས་གསུམ་གྱི་ཁྱད་པར་དང་ལྡན་པ་དེ་ནི་གནད་གལ་པོ་ཆེ་རུ་ཤེས་དགོས། དེས་ན་འཆར་ལུགས་ཤར་དང་འདྲ་ནའང་། གང་ཤར་ཐམས་ཅད་རང་ཤར་རང་གྲོལ་དུ་འགྲོ་བའི་གྲོལ་ལུགས་ཀྱི་ཁྱད་ཆོས་འདི་མེད་ན་སྒོམ་པ་འཁྲུལ་བའི་ལམ་ཡིན་ཏེ། ཇི་སྐད་དུ། སྒོམ་པ་ཤེས་ཀྱང་གྲོལ་མ་ཤེས། །བསམ་གཏན་ལྷ་དང་ཅི་མ་འདྲ། །ཞེས་དང་། ཞབས་དཀར་པས། གནས་པ་ཙམ་ནི་བསམ་གཏན་ལྷ་དང་འདྲ། །འགྱུ་བ་ཙམ་ནི་ཐ་མལ་ཤེས་པ་འདྲ། །དེ་ལ་བསྒོམས་ཀྱང་སངས་རྒྱས་ཐོབ་མི་འགྱུར། །ཞེས་པ་ལྟར། གནས་པ་ཙམ་དང་། གནས་འགྱུ་ངོ་ཤེས་པ་ཙམ་དང་། སྟོང་པར་རྒྱས་འདེབས་པ་ཙམ་ནི་གོལ་ས་གསུམ་ཡིན་ཏེ། སྒོམ་སེམས་གནས་ཀྱི་བསམ་གཏན་ཙམ་ལ་གདེང་བཅས་ན། དེའི་འབྲས་བུ་ཤི་མ་ཐག་ཏུ་ཁམས་གོང་མའི་བསམ་གཏན་དུ་སྐྱེ། གནས་འགྱུ་ངོ་ཤེས་པ་ཙམ་མ་གཏོགས་མེད་ན་དེ་ནི་འཁྲུལ་རྟོག་ཐ་མལ་གྱི་ཤེས་པ་ཡིན་པས་སོ་སོའི་སྐྱེ་བོའི་སེམས་དང་ཁྱད་པར་མེད། ཐམས་ཅད་སྟོང་པའོ་བསམས་ནས་བློས་བྱས་ཀྱིས་རྒྱས་འདེབས་པ་ནི། སྟོང་ཉིད་རྒྱས་འདེབས་སུ་ཤོར་བ་རྐྱེན་ངན་དང་འཕྲད་ཆེ་རྟོག་པའི་དུག་རོ་བསླང་འོང་སྟེ། ཇི་སྐད་དུ། ལྟོ་འགྲང་ཉེ་མས་དྲོས་ཆེ་ཆོས་པའི་གཟུགས། །རྐྱེན་ངན་ཐོག་ཏུ་བབས་ཆེ་ཐ་མལ་པ། །ཞེས་དང་། ལྟ་བ་ཀ་ཀན་གྱི་ཀ་བྱས་ན། །སྤྱོད་པ་བསྡམ་ཀན་གྱིས་བསྡམ་འོང་། ། ཞེས་སོ། །གཞིའི་བཞུགས་ཚུལ་ཡེ་ནས་འཕོ་འགྱུར་མེད་པས་ཡེ་གྲོལ། གང་ཟག་གི་སྣང་ཚུལ་ཡང་མཐའ་བཞིའི་འཛིན་སྟངས་དབྱིངས་སུ་ནུབ་པའི་མཐའ་གྲོལ། རིག་པ་སྐྱིང་དབུས་སུ་སད་ཆེ་གང་ཤར་གྱི་རྟོག་ཚོགས་ཐམས་ཅད་བག་བསག་ཡོད་མེད་པར་གྲོལ་བ་རང་གྲོལ། སྣང་བ་མ་སྤྱངས་སྣང་ཐོག་ཏུ་གྲོལ། འགྱུ་བ་མ་སྤྱངས་འགྱུ་ཐོག་ཏུ་གྲོལ་བ་ཅེར་གྲོལ་ཏེ་གྲོལ་

ཚུལ་བཞིའོ། །དེའང་རང་གྲོལ་མཉམ་བཞག་དང་ཧིང་ངེ་འཛིན་གྱི་རྒྱ་མ་
རལ་ན། ཅེར་གྲོལ་རྗེས་ཐོབ་ལ་བཞག་ནའང་ཆོག་གསུངས། ད་དུང་
གཅིག་གྲོལ་ལ་སོགས་མིང་ཇི་ལྟར་བཏགས་ཀྱང་མདོར་ན་རྣམ་རྟོག་རང་གྲོལ་
རྗེས་མེད་དུ་དག་པའི་གྲོལ་ཚུལ་འདི་དང་ལྡན་ན། ཉོན་མོངས་པ་དང་རྣམ་
རྟོག་གང་སྐྱེས་ཆོས་སྐུར་ལྡོང་ནས་འཁྲུལ་རྟོག་ཡེ་ཤེས་སུ་དག །རྐྱེན་ངན་
གྲོགས་སུ་ཤར། ཉོན་མོངས་པ་ལམ་དུ་བྱེད། འཁོར་བ་མ་སྤངས་རང་
སར་གྲོལ། སྲིད་ཞིའི་འཆིང་བ་ལས་གྲོལ་ཏེ། ཡེ་གྲོལ་ཀ་དག་ཆེན་པོ་
མ་བསྒོམས་ཆོས་སྐུའི་ངང་དུ་འདུ་འབྲལ་མེད་པར་གཏན་སྲིད་ཟིན་པ་ཡིན་
ནོ། །དེས་ན་འདིར་ཉོན་མོངས་པ་ཉན་ཐོས་ལྟར་མི་སྤང་། བྱང་སེམས་
ལྟར་མི་སྦྱོང་། སྔགས་ལྟར་མི་བསྒྱུར། གང་ཤར་རང་གྲོལ་ཆེན་པོའི་
ངང་བསྐྱང་བ་ནི་རང་བཞིན་རྫོགས་པ་ཆེན་པོའི་ཁྱད་ཆོས་ཡིན་ནོ། །དེ་ལྟ་
བུའི་གྲོལ་ལུགས་ཀྱི་གདེང་འདི་མེད་ན་ལྟ་བ་མཐོ་མཐོ་དང་། སྒོམ་པ་ཟབ་
ཟབ་ཇི་ལྟ་བུ་རྒྱུད་ན་ཡོད་ཀྱང་སེམས་ལ་མི་ཕན། ཉོན་མོངས་པའི་གཉེན་
པོར་མི་འགྲོ་བས་ན་ཡང་དག་པའི་ལམ་མ་ཡིན། རང་ཤར་རང་གྲོལ་གྱི་
གནད་འདི་དང་ལྡན་ན། ལྟ་བ་མཐོ་མཐོའི་འཛིན་སྟངས་དང་། སྒོམ་པ་
ཟབ་ཟབ་ཀྱི་གཏད་སོ་མེད་ཀྱང་། རང་རྒྱུད་གཉིས་འཛིན་གྱི་འཆིང་བ་ལས་
མི་གྲོལ་མི་སྲིད། གསེར་གླིང་ནས་ས་རྡོ་ཕལ་པ་བཙལ་ཀྱང་མི་རྙེད་པ་ལྟར།
གནས་འགྱུ་དང་རྣམ་རྟོག་གང་སྐྱེས་སྒོམ་དུ་ཤར་ནས། འཁྲུལ་བ་རང་
མཚན་པ་བཙལ་ཀྱང་མི་རྙེད་པར་འགྱུར་བས་ན། འདི་ཁོ་ན་ཉམས་ལེན་
གནད་དུ་འགྲོ་མི་འགྲོ་ལ་ལྟོས་ཏེ། ཤན་འབྱེད་ཀྱི་གནམ་ཐིག་ལྟ་བུ་ཡིན།
དེ་བཞིན་དུ་སྤྱོད་པས་ཚད་འཛིན་པ་ནི། འཁོར་བ་ལ་ངེས་འབྱུང་། རྒྱུ་
འབྲས་ལ་ཡིད་ཆེས། སེམས་ཅན་ལ་སྙིང་རྗེ། གནས་ཚུལ་ལ་དག་
སྣང་། བླ་མ་ལ་མོས་གུས། མཆེད་གྲོགས་ལ་བརྩེ་གདུང་།
བསྒོམས་བྱུང་གི་ཤེས་རབ་སོགས་ཡོད་མེད་ཀྱིས་ཤེས་སོ། །དེ་ལྟར་ལྟ་བའི་

སྙིང་ནས། ཉིན་མཚན་མེད་པར་སྒོམ་པའི་རྒྱུན་བསྲིངས་ཏེ། སྤྱར་བླ་མས་ངོ་སྤྲད་པ་དེའི་སྙིང་དུ་གདེང་གྲོལ་ཐོག་ཏུ་བཅའ་བ་སྟེ་གནད་ཀྱི་གསང་ཚིག་གསུམ་པའོ།། ༄ དེ་ནི་ལྟ་སྒོམ་སྤྱོད་གསུམ་གྱི་དོན་བསྡུས་ནི། སྤྱིར་རང་བཞིན་རྫོགས་པ་ཆེན་པོ་ལ་ལྟ་བ་དང་། སྒོམ་པ། སྤྱོད་པ། གསུམ་དང་། ད་ལྟ་ནས་སྐུ་གསུམ་གྱི་བསྒྲུབ་གཞིའི་འབྲས་བུ་དང་བཞི། དེ་ལས་མི་འདའ་བའི་དམ་ཚིག་དང་ལྔ་པོ་རིག་པ་ཟང་ཐལ་གཅིག་གི་སྙིང་ནས་བཞག་དགོས། དེ་བཞིན་དུ་གཞི་ལམ་འབྲས་གསུམ་ཀྱང་རིག་པ་གཅིག་ལས་གཞན་མེད་དེ། གཉུག་མའི་ཡེ་ཤེས་དེ་ཉིད་རང་རྒྱུད་ལ་ཡེ་ནས་བཞུགས་པའི་ཆ་ནས་གཞི་དང་། ད་ལྟ་བླ་མས་ངོ་སྤྲད་དེ་ཉམས་སུ་ལེན་པའི་ཆ་ནས་ལམ། ཉམས་སུ་བླངས་ནས་སྒྲིབ་གཉིས་གཞི་ཀློང་དུ་དེངས་པའི་ཆ་ནས་འབྲས་བུ་ཡིན་ནོ། །འོན་ཀྱང་གཞུང་ལུགས་སྤྱིའི་གཏན་ལ་དབབ་ཚུལ་ལྟར་ཆོས་ཐམས་ཅད་ལུང་རིགས་དང་གཏན་ཚིགས་ཀྱིས་གཞལ་ནས་གཏན་ལ་འབེབས་ཚུལ་ལྟར་མ་ཡིན་པར་རང་རྒྱུད་ལ་ཡེ་ནས་གནས་པའི་གཉུག་མ་དོན་གྱི་ཡེ་ཤེས་དེ་ཉིད་ད་ལྟ་བླ་མའི་མན་ངག་གིས་སད་པར་བྱས་ཏེ་མངོན་སུམ་རིག་ཆ་རྗེན་པའི་དོན་ཐོག་ཏུ་ངོ་སྤྲད་དེ། ཕུ་ཐག་ནང་ནས་ཆོད། ཡིན་མིན་གྱི་སྒྲོག་ལས་གྲོལ་བ་ཞིག་བྱུང་ན་ལྟ་བ་དེ་ཡིན། དེས་ན་ཨ་ཏི་ཡོ་ག་ཁྲིགས་ཆོད་ཀྱི་ལྟ་བ་འདི་ཉིད་ཉམས་སུ་ལེན་པ་ལ། ན་སོ་རྒན་གཞོན། ཤེས་རབ་ཆེ་ཆུང་། དབང་པོ་རྣོ་རྟུལ། ལས་བཟང་ངན་སོགས་ལ་མི་ལྟོས་པར། དད་པ་དང་། མོས་གུས། བརྩོན་འགྲུས་ལ་བརྟེན་ནས། རང་བྱུང་རིག་པ་གང་ཟག་སུ་ཞིག་གིས་རྟོགས་ན་དེ་ཉིད་གྲོལ་བ་ཡིན་ནོ།། ༄ གསུམ་པ་མཇུག་གི་དོན་ལ། དོན་བསྡུ་བ། གདམས་པ་ཤིན་ཏུ་ཟབ་པར་གདམས་པ། རྗེས་ཆེ་བ་བཀའ་རྒྱས་གདབ་པ་དང་གསུམ་ལས། དང་པོ་ནི། གནད་གསུམ་ལྡན་པའི་ལྟ་བ་ལ། །མཁྱེན་བརྩེ་འབྲེལ་བའི་སྒོམ་པ་དང་། །རྒྱལ་སྲས་སྤྱི་ཡི་

སྤྱོད་པ་གྲོགས། །དེ་ལྟར་ངོ་རང་ཐོག་ཏུ་སྤྲད་པ། ཐག་གཅིག་ཐོག་ཏུ་བཅད་པ། གདེང་གྲོལ་ཐོག་ཏུ་བཅའ་བ་སྟེ་གནད་གསུམ་ག་དང་ལྡན་པའི་ལྟ་བ་འདི་ནི་ཐེག་དགུའི་ཡང་རྩེ་འབྲས་བུའི་ཐེག་པའི་ལྟ་བ་ཡིན་པ་དང་། དཔེར་ན་རིའི་རྒྱལ་པོ་མཆོག་རབ་དེ་འཇིག་རྟེན་ཁམས་ཀྱི་རི་ཐམས་ཅད་ཀྱི་ཡང་རྩེར་སོན་པ་དང་། རིའི་རྒྱལ་པོ་ཡིན་པ་བཞིན་དུ། ཐེག་པ་འདིའང་ཐེག་པ་ཐམས་ཅད་ཀྱི་རྒྱལ་པོ་ཡིན་པས་ན། ལྟ་བུ་འདི་ལ་འོག་མའི་ཐེག་པ་ཐམས་ཅད་ནམ་ཞིག་སྦྱོར་བར་མ་ནུས་ན་འབྲས་བུ་སངས་རྒྱས་ཀྱི་གོ་འཕང་ཐོབ་མི་སྲིད་པ་དང་། ཐེག་པ་ཐམས་ཅད་འདིའི་ལམ་སྐེགས་སམ་གྲོགས་སུ་འགྲོ་ཚུལ་ཡང་། དཔེར་ན་འཁོར་ལོ་སྒྱུར་བའི་རྒྱལ་པོ་གང་དུ་བྱོན་ཀྱང་རྒྱལ་སྲིད་བདུན་དང་འཁོར་ཡན་ལག་གི་དཔུང་ཚོགས་མེད་མི་སྲིད་དེ། སྡུད་པ་ལས། འཁོར་ལོ་སྒྱུར་རྒྱལ་ལམ་གང་ནས་ནི་རྟག་འགྲོ་བ། །ལམ་དེ་ཉིད་ནས་རིན་ཆེན་བདུན་དང་དཔུང་ཚོགས་ཀུན། །གང་ནས་རྒྱལ་བའི་ཤེས་རབ་ཕ་རོལ་ཕྱིན་འདི་འགྲོ། དེ་ཉིད་ནས་ནི་ཡོན་ཏན་ཆོས་ཀུན་འགྲོ་བར་འགྱུར། །ཞེས་གསུངས་པ་ལྟར། ཐེག་པ་ཐམས་ཅད་འདི་ཉིད་ཀྱི་ཡན་ལག་ཡིན་པ་དང་། འདི་ཉིད་རྟོགས་བྱེད་ཀྱི་གྲོགས་སུ་འགྲོ་བ་ཡིན། སྤྱིར་ཀ་དག་ཁྲེགས་ཆོད་ཀྱི་རིག་པ་དང་། ལྷུན་གྲུབ་ཐོད་རྒལ་གྱི་ཤེས་རབ་རང་བྱུང་གི་སྒྲོན་མ་གཉིས་དོན་གཅིག་ཡིན་པས་ན། ཀ་དག་རིག་པ་ནི་ཤེས་རབ་རང་བྱུང་སྒྲོན་མའི་ངོ་བོ་ཡིན། དེའི་གདངས་རྡོ་རྗེ་ལུ་གུ་རྒྱུད། རྩལ་བསྒོམས་བྱུང་གི་ཤེས་རབ་ཡིན། དེས་ན་རིག་ངོ་འཕྲོད་ཅིང་དེ་ལ་གོམས་འདྲིས་སོང་བ་ན། རྩལ་བསྒོམས་བྱུང་གི་ཤེས་རབ་འབར་ནས། ཆོས་ཅན་གྱི་སྣང་ཚུལ་དང་། ཆོས་ཉིད་ཀྱི་གནས་ལུགས་ཇི་ལྟ་བ་བཞིན་དུ་མཁྱེན་པའི་ཀློང་དབྱར་གྱི་ཆུ་མཚོ་བཞིན་དུ་རྫོལ་བ་དང་། སྟོང་ཉིད་སྙིང་རྗེའི་སྙིང་པོ་ཅན་དུ་ཤར་ཏེ་འདི་ཉིད་མ་རྟོགས་པའི་སེམས་ཅན་ལ་བརྩེ་བའི་སྙིང་རྗེ་རྩོལ་མེད་དུ་འབྱུང་བ་དང་། དེ་ལྟར་རྣམ་ཀུན་མཆོག་ལྡན་གྱི་སྟོང་ཉིད་

དམ་གདོད་མའི་སྟོང་ཆེན་གྱི་དབྱིངས་དེ་ཉིད་དང་། བརྩེ་པའི་སྙིང་རྗེ་ཆེན་པོ་གཉིས་ཟུང་དུ་འཇུག་པའམ། དེ་གཉིས་འབྲེལ་བའི་སྒོམ་པའི་ངང་བསྐྱང་རྒྱུ་དེ་སྒོམ་པ་ཡིན་པ་དང་། དེ་ལྟར་སྟོང་ཉིད་སྙིང་རྗེ་ཟུང་དུ་འཇུག་པའི་ལམ་གནད་མངོན་དུ་གྱུར་ཅོ། མཉམ་བཞག་ཏུ་དམིགས་མེད་ཡེ་ཤེས་ཀྱི་ཚོགས་དང་། རྗེས་ཐོབ་ཏུ་དམིགས་བཅས་བསོད་ནམས་ཀྱི་ཚོགས་རྒྱལ་སྲས་སྤྱོའི་སྤྱོད་པ་ཕ་རོལ་ཏུ་ཕྱིན་པ་དྲུག་སོགས་སྤྱོད་པ་རྒྱ་མཚོ་ལྟ་བུ་རིག་པའི་རྩལ་རོལ་བ་ལས་ཤར་བ་ནི། དཔེར་ན་ཉི་མ་དང་། ཉི་མའི་འོད་ཟེར་ལྟར་འཕྲོ་བ་འདི་ཞི་མཐའ་འགོག་བྱེད་ཀྱི་གྲོགས་སུ་ཤར་བའོ།། ༄

གཉིས་པ་གདམས་པ་ཤིན་ཏུ་ཟབ་པར་གདམས་པ་ནི། དུས་གསུམ་རྒྱལ་བའི་ཞལ་བསྟུར་ཀྱང་། །འདི་ལས་ལྷག་པའི་གདམས་ངག་མེད། །རིག་རྩལ་ཆོས་སྐུའི་གཏེར་སྟོན་གྱིས། །ཤེས་རབ་ཀློང་ནས་གཏེར་དུ་བླངས། །ས་རྟོའི་བཅུད་དང་འདི་མི་འདྲ། །དགའ་རབ་རྡོ་རྗེའི་ཞལ་ཆེམས་ཡིན། །བརྒྱུད་པ་གསུམ་གྱི་ཐུགས་བཅུད་ཡིན། །དེ་ལྟ་བུའི་གདམས་ངག་ཚིག་གསུམ་གནད་དུ་རྡེག་པ་འདི་ནི་འདས་མ་འོངས་ད་ལྟ་དུས་གསུམ་གྱི་རྒྱལ་བ་ཐམས་ཅད་ཀྱི་བཀའ་གྲོས་མཛད་དེ་ཞལ་བསྡུར་ནའང་འདི་ལས་ཟབ་པ་ཞིག་མེད་དེ། འདི་ནི་དུས་གསུམ་གྱི་སངས་རྒྱས་ཐམས་ཅད་ཀྱི་དགོངས་པ། མ་མཁའ་འགྲོ་འབུམ་གྱི་སྙིང་ཁྲག །ཆོས་ཕྱུང་བརྒྱད་ཁྲི་བཞི་སྟོང་གི་ཡང་སྙིང་། ཐེག་པ་ཐམས་ཅད་ཀྱི་རྩེ་རྒྱལ། རྒྱུད་སྡེ་ཐམས་ཅད་ཀྱི་སྙིང་ཕྱུང་བ་ལྟ་བུ། མན་ངག་ཐམས་ཅད་ཀྱི་བཅུད་བསྡུས་པ། གསུང་རབ་ཐམས་ཅད་ཀྱི་གནད་དྲིལ་བ། འོ་མ་བསྲུབས་པ་ལས་མར་གྱི་ཉིང་ཁུ་འབྱུང་བ་ལྟ་བུ་ཡིན་ནོ། །དེས་ན་འོད་གསལ་རྫོགས་པ་ཆེན་པོ་ཀློང་ཆེན་སྙིང་ཐིག་གི་དོན་གནད་སྨན་གྱི་ཐུས་ཀ་ལྟར་ཕྱོགས་གཅིག་ཏུ་བསྡུས་པ་འདི་ལས་ལྷག་པའི་གདམས་ངག་རྗོད་བྱེད་ཚིག་ཉུང་ལ། བརྗོད་བྱ་དོན་ཟབ་པ་ཞིག་གཞན་ན་མེད་དོ། །ཨ་བུ་རིན་པོ་ཆེའི་ཁོང་གི་རིག་པའི་རྩལ་ལས་

ཤར་བ་དགོངས་གཏེར་གྱི་ཚུལ་དུ་ཐབ་པས་ན་ཆོས་སྐུའི་གཏེར་སྟོན་གྱི་ཐ་སྙད་སྦྱར་བ་དང་། ཁོང་གིས་ཐུགས་ཁྱབ་གདལ་ནམ་མཁའ་ལྟ་བུའི་བདག་མེད་རྟོགས་པའི་ཤེས་རབ་ཀྱི་ཀློང་ནས་གང་ཤར་ཐོལ་བྱུང་གི་ཚུལ་དུ་གསུངས་པས་ན་གཏེར་དུ་བླངས་པའི་ཐ་སྙད་སྦྱར་བ་དང་། འཇིག་རྟེན་པའི་ནོར་གཏེར་སུ་རྫའི་བཅུད་དུ་སྨིན་པ་དག་གིས་ཀྱང་ཚེ་འདིར་རྒུད་པ་སེལ་བ་དང་། དབུལ་བ་སེལ་བ་ལྟ་བུ་འཕྲུལ་དུ་ནུས་པ་ཐོན་པ་ཡོད་ཀྱང་། དེ་དག་དང་འདྲེ་ཉིད་མི་འདྲ་གསུངས། དེའི་ཚུལ་ཡང་ཉག་བླ་བསོད་རྒྱལ་གྱི་ཞལ་ནས། ངས་ཨ་བུ་རིན་པོ་ཆེ་ལ་གཏེར་སྒྲོམ་ཞིག་ཕུལ་བར། ཁོང་གིས་ཐུགས་དགྱེས་ཚུལ་མ་མཛད་ནས་འདི་སྐད་གསུངས། འདི་འདྲ་དེ་ཡོན་ཀྱང་ཆོག་ལ་མ་ཡོན་ཀྱང་ཆོག ཇི་ལྟར་ཡིན་ཞེ་ན། མ་རིག་བདེན་འཛིན་གྱིས་བྲངས་པའི་དུག་གསུམ་ཡིད་ཀྱི་འཁྲུལ་རྟོག་འདི་དམར་པོ་བྲག་གི་རྫོང་བས་ཀྱང་སྲ། ཉམས་བདེ་གསལ་མི་རྟོག་གསུམ་པོ་སྟོན་མོ་ཆུ་ཡི་རྒྱ་མཚོ་ལས་གཏིང་ཟབ། རྒྱ་འདི་གཏོར་དཀའ། གཏིང་འདི་ཕུག་དཀའ། དེས་ན་བླ་མ་དམ་པའི་མན་ངག་དང་ཤེས་རབ་གཟེར་གྱིས་མ་རིག་བདེན་འཛིན་གྱིས་བྲངས་པའི་དུག་གསུམ་ཡིད་ཀྱི་འཁྲུལ་རྟོག་གི་བྲག་རི་འདི་གཏོར། ཉམས་བདེ་གསལ་མི་རྟོག་གསུམ་སྟོན་མོ་ཆུའི་རྒྱ་མཚོ་ལྟ་བུའི་གཏིང་འདི་ཟང་ཐལ་དུ་ཕུག་སྟེ། དེ་ཕན་ཆད་ན་ཀུན་གཞི་ཚོགས་བརྒྱད་ཀྱི་སྒྲོམ་ནས་རང་བྱུང་གི་ཡེ་ཤེས་རྗེན་པ་ཀུན་ཏུ་བཟང་པོའི་དགོངས་པ་མཐར་ཐུག་པ་དེ་བླངས་བ་ནི་དོན་དམ་པའི་གཏེར་ཡིན། གཏེར་དེ་འདྲ་བླངས་ན་ངོ་མཚར་ཆེ། ཞེས་གསུངས་སོ། །རིག་འཛིན་དགའ་རབ་རྡོ་རྗེ་ཆུ་བོ་ཏན་ཏིག་གི་མགུལ་དུ་སྐུ་མྱ་ངན་ལས་འདས་ཚེ། སློབ་དཔོན་འཇམ་དཔལ་བཤེས་གཉེན་གྱིས་གདུང་ཆེག་གིས་གསོལ་བ་བཏབ་པ་ན། འཇའ་འོད་ཁ་དོག་ལྔ་ལྡན་གྱི་ཀློང་ནས་སློབ་དཔོན་དགའ་རབ་རྡོ་རྗེའི་ཡེ་ཤེས་སྒྱུ་མའི་སྐུའི་ཕྱག་གཡས་པའི་གྲུ་མོ་མན་ཆད་བྱུང་ནས། རིན་པོ་ཆེ་སྣ་ལྔའི་སྒྲོམ་བུའི་ནང་དུ། བཻཌཱུརྻའི་ཤོག་གུ་ལ

གསེར་གྱི་ཞུན་མའི་ཡི་གེ་རང་བྱུང་དུ་བྲིས་པའི་ཚིག་གསུམ་གནད་དུ་བརྡེག་པའི་ཞལ་ཆེམས་འདི་བྱུང་བ་ཡིན། སློབ་དཔོན་འཇམ་དཔལ་བཤེས་གཉེན་གྱིས་མཐོང་བ་ཙམ་གྱིས་དཔོན་སློབ་དགོངས་པ་དབྱེར་མེད་དུ་འདྲེས་པ་ཡིན། དེ་ལྟ་བུའི་གདམས་ངག་ཟབ་མོ་འདི་ཉིད་ཀྱི་དོན་ཇི་ལྟ་བ་བཞིན་དུ་རྒྱུད་ལ་རྟོགས་པ། ཀུན་མཁྱེན་ཆོས་ཀྱི་རྒྱལ་པོ་ཀློང་ཆེན་རབ་འབྱམས་དེ་ཉིད་སྐུ་ཚེ་དེ་ཉིད་ལ་ཆོས་ཟད་ཀྱི་དགོངས་པ་མངོན་དུ་གྱུར་ནས་མངོན་པར་རྫོགས་པར་སངས་རྒྱས་ཏེ། སྐུ་མྱ་ངན་ལས་འདས་ཚེ་གདུང་དང་རིང་བསྲེལ་འགྲོ་བའི་མཆོད་སྡོང་དུ་བཞག་པ་དེ། རྒྱལ་བ་དགོངས་པའི་བརྒྱུད་པ་དང་། ཀུན་མཁྱེན་མྱ་ངན་ལས་འདས་ཏེ་ལོ་ལྔ་བརྒྱ་ལྷག་སོང་བའི་རྗེས་སུ་རིག་འཛིན་འཇིགས་མེད་གླིང་པའི་བསམ་ཡས་འཆིམས་ཕུ་ནགས་ཀྱི་འདབས་སུ་ལོ་གསུམ་དུ་སྒྲུབ་པ་མཛད་སྐབས། ཀུན་མཁྱེན་ཆེན་པོར་གསོལ་བ་རྩེ་གཅིག་ཏུ་བཏབ། བླ་སྒྲུབ་ཐིག་ལེའི་རྒྱ་ཅན་ལ་བརྟེན་ནས། ཀུན་མཁྱེན་ཆེན་པོའི་ཡེ་ཤེས་སྒྱུ་མའི་སྐུས་ལན་གསུམ་ལ་ཞལ་གཟིགས། དེ་ནི་རིག་འཛིན་བརྡའི་བརྒྱུད་པ་ཡིན། དེས་འཇིགས་མེད་རྒྱལ་བའི་མྱུ་གུ་ལ་གདམས་ཏེ་ཆོས་ཉིད་མངོན་སུམ་དུ་མཇལ་བ་དེ་ནི་གང་ཟག་སྙན་ཁུང་གི་བརྒྱུད་པ་ཡིན། དེས་ན་བརྒྱུད་པ་གསུམ་གྱི་ཐུགས་བཅུད་ཡིན་ཚུལ་དེ་ལྟར་རོ།། ༈ གསུམ་པ་རྩིས་ཆེ་བར་བཀའ་རྒྱས་གདབ་པ་ནི། སྙིང་གི་བུ་ལ་གཏད་དོ་རྒྱ། །ཟབ་དོན་ཡིན་ནོ་སྙིང་གི་གཏམ། །སྙིང་གཏམ་ཡིན་ནོ་དོན་གྱི་གནད། །དོན་གནད་ཡལ་བར་མ་དོར་ཅིག །གདམས་ངག་ཟགས་སུ་མ་འཇུག་ཅིག །མཁས་པ་ཤྲཱི་རྒྱལ་པོའི་ཁྲིད་ཆོས་སོ། །ཞེས་དེ་ལྟ་བུའི་མན་ངག་ཟབ་མོ་སྙིང་གི་ཐིག་ལེ་ལྟ་བུ་འདི་ཉམས་སུ་མི་ལེན་པའི་སྣོད་མིན་ལ་བསྟན་དུ་མི་རུང་ཞིང་། སྣོད་ལྡན་གྱི་གང་ཟག་གདམས་ངག་མིག་འབྲས་བཞིན་གཅེས་པའི་སྐྱེས་བུ་རྣམས་ལ་མ་བསྟན་ན་ཕངས་བས་ན། སྐལ་ལྡན་གྱི་སློབ་མ་སྙིང་གི་བུ་ལྟ་བུ་རྣམས་ལ་བརྩེ་བའི་སྒོ་ནས་གཏད་དོ་ཞེས། གཏད་

པའི་དོན་ནི་སྣོད་མིན་རྣམས་ལ་མི་སྟོན་པར་གསང་རྒྱ་མཛོད་ལ་རང་གིས་ཉམས་སུ་ལོངས་ཤིག །འདི་ནི་གསང་བ་ཟབ་མོའི་དོན་རྣམས་ཕྱོགས་གཅིག་ཏུ་བསྡུས་ཏེ་ཚིག་ཉུང་ལ་དོན་འདུས་ཤིང་ཞལ་གསལ་བར་བྱས་ནས་བསྟན་པ་ཡིན་ནོ། །ཞེས་ཁོང་གི་སྐལ་ལྡན་གྱི་སློབ་མ་སྣོད་ལྡན་གྱི་གང་ཟག་རྣམས་ལ་སྙིང་གི་གཏམ་རྗེན་བྱུང་བྱུས་ནས་གསུངས་པ་ཡིན། གདམས་ངག་འདི་ནི་དཔྲལ་བའི་མིག་དང་ཁོག་པའི་སྙིང་བཞིན་དུ་ཕངས་ཤིང་གཅེས་ནོར་ཡིན་པས་ན་སྙིང་གཏམ་ཡིན་ནོ། །ཀུན་མཁྱེན་ཆེན་པོའི་སྙན་བརྒྱུད་སྐོར་གསུམ་གྱི་དོན་གནད་ཀྱང་འདིར་འདུས་པས་ན་དོན་གྱི་གནད། དེ་ལྟ་བུའི་དོན་གནད་ཟབ་མོ་དགོས་འདོད་ཀུན་འབྱུང་གི་ནོར་བུ་ལྟ་བུ་འདི་གཅེས་སྤྲས་ཀྱིས་ཉམས་སུ་མི་ལེན་པར་དགོས་མེད་ཡལ་བར་མ་དོར་ཅིག །གདམས་ངག་ཟབ་མོ་སྨན་འཆི་གསོས་ཀྱི་བདུད་རྩི་ལྟ་བུ་འདི་རང་གི་རྣ་ལམ་དུ་ཐོས་ཀྱང་རྩེ་གཅིག་ཏུ་ཉམས་སུ་མ་བླངས་ན་སྣོད་ཆག་ནས་བཅུད་ཟགས་སུ་བཅུག་པ་དང་འདྲ་བས། དེ་ལྟར་ཟགས་སུ་མ་འཇུག་ཅིག །མདོ་སྔགས་རིག་གནས་དང་བཅས་པའི་གཙུག་ལག་རྒྱ་མཚོ་ལྟ་བུའི་ཕ་རོལ་དུ་སོན་པ་མཁས་པ་ཤྲཱིའམ་དཔལ་རྒྱལ་པོའི་ཁྱད་ཆོས་སུ་བརྗོད་པ་རྫོགས་སོ།། །། །ཞེས་པའང་བླ་མ་དམ་པ་རྣམས་ཀྱི་ཞལ་རྒྱུན་དང་རང་གིས་གང་དྲན་ཡིག་ཐོག་ཏུ་བཀོད་པ་ཡིན་ཀྱང་། རང་ལ་ཡོན་ཏན་ཅི་ཡང་མེད་པས་དམ་པ་རྣམས་ཀྱི་ཐུགས་ཁྲེལ་བའི་རྒྱུ་རུ་ཨེ་འགྲོ་སྙམ་ནས་སྐྲག་འཛིགས་སྐྱེ་བའི་གནས་སུ་འདུག་མོད། འོན་ཀྱང་རང་གི་ཚ་བུ་དམ་པ་ཚུལ་ཁྲིམས་བཟང་པོ་དང་། སྨོན་ལས་ཀྱིས་འབྲེལ་བའི་ཨ་བུ་དཀར་ལོ། ཚ་བུ་རྣམ་འདྲེན། མཁན་ཐུབ་ཆོས། ཆོས་གྲོགས་བློ་གྲོས་རྣམས་ཀྱིས་ནན་བསྐུལ་མ་བཟློད་པར་སྤྲང་འཁྱམ་པ་བསྟན་མེད་པས་སོ། །དགེའོ། །དགེའོ། །དགེའོ། །

སརྦ་མངྒ་ལཾ།།

INDEX